TIMELESS PRINCIPLES OF FINANCIAL SECURITY

Laura,

I really enjoyed speaking with you. It sounds like Bob + Peggy Demars were really lucky to find you. Hope you enjoy the book, and I look forward to reading yours!

—Adam

TIMELESS PRINCIPLES OF FINANCIAL SECURITY

FINDING PEACE AND PROSPERITY IN AN UNCERTAIN WORLD

ADAM DAWSON, CFP®

Printed in the United States of America

ISBN-13: 978-0615649160

ISBN-10: 0615649165

*For my dear wife Andrea, whose lifelong comfort and happiness
I hope to secure through living these principles.*

Acknowledgments

Many great minds have contributed either directly or indirectly to the content of this book. Words cannot express my gratitude for the many valuable lessons I have learned over the years from teachers, colleagues, clients, friends, family members, spiritual leaders, authors, historians, philosophers, and others. Thank you for teaching me timeless principles of financial security so I could apply them for the benefit of my family and share them with others.

I deeply appreciate those who gave much of their time to provide important insight during the editing stages of the manuscript. I would also like to thank my wife and children for their patience while I worked on this book over the past year-and-a-half. I could not have done it without their support, and I am sure they are even happier than I am that it is finally finished!

Thanks also to my clients, several of whom have become good friends. I treasure my association with you and have learned more from many of you than you may ever realize. Thank you for your continued confidence in me and for allowing me to succeed in a profession I love so dearly.

Contents

Introduction

The Purpose of This Book

Would you like to become a multi-millionaire overnight? Are you searching for the secret formulas that will double the value of your investments every year? If so, you are reading the wrong book.

This is not a book about how to get rich quickly. My purpose is to help you obtain lasting financial security and eliminate your fear of running out of money so you can accomplish your most important priorities in life.

I have experienced the desperate feeling of not having any money, and it is not fun. Throughout my childhood my family was very poor, but when I was ten years old my parents divorced and things turned from bad to worse. In an effort to improve our situation, my mother took my three younger siblings and me across the country by train to start working on her master's degree. The five of us moved into a tiny run-down apartment with no furniture. Since we could not take much with us on the train and could not afford to replace what we left behind, for a while we slept on the floor and took turns eating meals with the one plate, one cup, one bowl, and one set of flatware we owned. We each had only a few sets of worn-out hand-me-down clothes to wear, which we washed by hand in the bathtub. We walked everywhere because we had no car. Our situation did not improve much for quite some time.

Although these were very difficult experiences that I would not wish on anyone, they taught me important lessons about the value of hard work, education, and thrift. They also enabled me to be more grateful for the success I have enjoyed as an adult and to feel more compassion for those who are tormented by money problems.

I do not fault my parents for the hardships we endured. They simply were doing the best they could with the knowledge they had. Even though they were ill-equipped to teach me about money, I am indebted to them for the many other even more important lessons they taught me. However, in college I set out on a mission to learn sound financial principles so my wife and children would not have to suffer in this way, and so I could help reduce suffering in the lives of others.

Successful money management has very little to do with math and everything to do with properly directing our attitudes, emotions, and behavior. It has very little to do with how much money we make and everything to do with how wisely we utilize what we receive.

Most financial problems stem from our tendency to trade what we want *most* for what we want *now* and from our subconscious belief that our income will always either remain level or increase. If our income ever drops even just by a little, many of us find ourselves in trouble.

Life is unpredictable. What do you fear might ruin your plans? Another stock market collapse? Another real estate crash? Higher taxes? Unemployment? Natural disasters? Hyperinflation? Skyrocketing health care costs? Evaporation of Social Security and Medicare benefits? Soaring nursing home costs? Law suit? Income loss due to serious illness or injury? Dying too soon? Outliving your retirement savings? Is it possible to obtain a reasonable level of certainty that you can maintain financial independence throughout your life despite all these and other looming threats?

People typically blame their financial woes on external forces over which they have no control. However, we do not have to be mere victims of circumstance. We must take responsibility for our own well-being by applying the timeless principles of financial security that successful people have relied on for generations. These principles can help us achieve and maintain prosperity and independence throughout our entire lives, regardless of economic reversals or personal tragedies which may threaten to financially devastate us.

Throughout this book I will define these principles and explore their practical application in our modern society. Although we will discuss many important principles, the most essential ones are summarized below:

1. Be honest in all financial dealings. Pay all obligations fully and on time.
2. Donate at least 10% of gross income to tithing or other charitable causes.
3. Fully protect assets and income through proper types and amounts of insurance.
4. Save at least 20% of gross income for the future before spending any of it.
5. Maintain at least three months' worth of liquid cash and food storage.
6. Ensure complementary balance among various investment objectives and methods of tax treatment.
7. Minimize investment risk, invest primarily in what you understand, and be content with modest gains.
8. Avoid and eliminate debt.
9. Work as long as your health permits, even if just part-time, and continually improve your education.
10. Leave a meaningful legacy. Organize and protect your estate with valid legal documents and properly titled assets.

My Role as an Advisor

As a CERTIFIED FINANCIAL PLANNER™ professional, I help people achieve and maintain financial security throughout their entire lives. This involves helping them understand and organize their personal finances, make wise investment and insurance decisions, and prepare for a secure retirement. My goal is to help as many people as possible avoid financial threats, fulfill their obligations, and capture opportunities that may come their way. CFP® certification requires rigorous training in every area of personal finance: investment management, retirement planning, insurance planning, tax planning, estate planning, and so on. Once certified, The Certified Financial Planner Board of Standards also requires CFP® professionals to regularly engage in continuing education, always put the best interest of the client first, and abide by the highest standards of integrity, objectivity, competence, fairness, confidentiality, professionalism, and diligence.

Many people employ several advisors who each excel at their specialty, but who never communicate with each other to ensure that their recommendations harmonize with one another. These advisors may include accountants, attorneys, auto insurance agents, life insurance agents, bankers, stock brokers, realtors, and others. Who is looking at the big picture to ensure all these advisors are working in harmony towards achieving the client's overall objectives? That is my role.

I *love* my job because I feel that I make a significant difference in people's lives by helping them obtain greater hope and freedom. Often our work together also enables them to become a greater benefit to other people. I have met many amazing people who do a lot of good in the world. It is an honor to play a small role in helping them fulfill their dreams.

Another thing I love about my job is that I often learn as much from the people I am helping as they learn from me. I have worked with many very successful people from whom I have learned excellent money management skills and attitudes. I also have learned a lot about what not to do from people who have endured great hardship as a result of less astute financial decisions.

Since I started my career in 2000, I have witnessed the impact of two major market melt-downs on many people. Some were well-prepared to weather the storm, while others lost everything. Through years of rigorous study and careful observation of how a great variety of people manage money, I have learned the timeless principles of financial security that can be relied upon in any economy. These principles can be difficult for the average person to discover on their own for three major reasons:

1. Those who succeed are often very private because they do not want to brag or become a target.
2. Those who fail are often too embarrassed to admit how badly they failed and why.
3. The noise of the media and the hype of hot new investment products often drown out all reason.

I hope that through this book you will benefit from what I have learned so you will have the knowledge and attitudes you need to be financially secure throughout your entire life.

As a religious person, I firmly believe that temporal and spiritual matters are directly related to each other. The two cannot really be separated. What we do with our time, abilities, and money is simply an outward manifestation of our love for God and other people, or lack thereof. Therefore, I believe that wise money management is just as much a spiritual issue as it is a secular issue.

I quote the Holy Bible several times throughout this book because I consider it to be an important authority on both spiritual and temporal matters. All such quotations will be from the Authorized King James Version. If you do not personally accept the Bible as an authority on these matters, please carefully consider the principles taught in these quotes and relate them to whatever religious text you do accept. I believe that when examined with an open mind, you will find them to be compatible with your beliefs.

How Do You Make Money Decisions?

Although money is a crucial part of everyone's life, most people do not seem to understand very much about how it works. The result is that many financial decisions—even huge, life-altering decisions—are made on a whim, based on convenience, emotions, or the misguided opinions of others.

These opinions may come from well-meaning family members, friends, or co-workers who know very little about personal finance. These opinions may also come from financial "experts" found in every form of media: books, magazines, newspapers, the internet, radio, or television.

Blindly following advice from these sources can be dangerous without also seeking the advice of a qualified professional. Often financial talking heads give exaggerated sweeping generalizations that are catered to the masses for the purpose of maximizing entertainment value and advertising revenue. They take no responsibility for how your life will turn out if you take their opinions to heart. Their advice cannot be tailored to your specific situation, personality, or goals. Just read or listen to the disclaimers typically found at the end of every article or show.

People who blindly follow the opinions of others often feel anxious, wondering for years whether they made the right decisions. Over time they are sure to hear conflicting opinions from other sources, telling them they should have done something else. If a course correction is necessary, it might be extremely expensive and in some cases may not even be possible.

Confidence that You Made the Right Decision

How can we make decisions free from bias, hype, and the opinions of others? How can we know that our choices are the best course for our unique objectives and personality? Can we possibly feel at peace about our financial decisions, regardless of who might try to pull us in other directions?

Yes, we can! The key is to make every decision in the context of the big picture. The first thing I do when I meet with new clients is help them organize their personal finances. Then I summarize everything about their current situation on one page and make sure they understand what they have, so they have a clear view of where they really are.

I encourage you to get organized, too. Think of it as a "You Are Here" sign on a mall directory. You cannot know how to get where you want to go until you know where you are.

To make it easy for people to see where they stand and where their strengths and weaknesses lie, I break down every aspect of their personal finances into four major categories:

1. Protection (insurance and legal documents)
2. Assets (savings and investments)
3. Liabilities (debts and taxes)
4. Cash Flow (income and expenses)

Most of us do not realize the impact each financial decision has on all four categories. This is because we think they are unrelated, and because most decisions tend to be reactive in nature. We have a baby, so we decide to buy a bigger house. Suddenly we face urgent decisions about homeowners insurance and what kind of mortgage to get without really knowing which is the best option for us, or caring how these decisions might impact our retirement savings, emergency cash, or other existing debts.

Over time we acquire many different financial products from various institutions, and each provider only asks questions directly related to their product. They seldom coordinate their recommendations with other aspects of our finances. This is why most people's finances are disorganized and inefficient.

When you last bought a new car did your insurance agent ask how much money you make or how much your investments are worth? When you enrolled in your 401(k) at work did your HR director ask about your monthly mortgage payment, how much you have in liquid savings, the interest rate on your credit card debt, or how much you paid in taxes last year?

Interdependent Financial Decisions

In reality, each category of our finances is *interdependent,* not independent of one another. This means that every decision we make in one category really does impact the other categories, whether or not we realize it.

How? If I were at fault in a serious automobile accident and did not have adequate insurance, I may be required to liquidate a significant amount of my investments to satisfy a judgment. The court may also decide to garnish my wages for several years, which might require me to wait much longer to retire or prohibit me from ever retiring. It may also reduce my current standard of living or increase my debt. So what does car insurance, which on the surface appears to be only a protection decision, have to do with my assets, liabilities, and cash flow? Everything!

Let's go back to the 401(k) example. An HR director probably would not even be allowed to ask about my mortgage payment, liquid savings, credit card debt, or taxes. However, would these questions be relevant to my decision whether to invest in a 401(k) and how much to contribute? Absolutely!

What if I only have $1,000 in liquid savings and my monthly mortgage payment is 30% of my gross monthly income? I may be better off putting the money in a liquid savings account to cover unexpected emergencies or unemployment, because I may not be able access my 401(k) for these purposes without significant penalties.

What if I have credit card debt at 18% interest and am only making the minimum payments? Then maybe I should pay off my credit card first, because I am highly unlikely to make anything close to 18% consistently on my 401(k) investments.

What if I am married with three kids, donate 10% of my income to my church, and own a home, so my itemized deductions already put me in a relatively low tax bracket? Then maxing out my 401(k) contribution just to get another tax deduction may not be the best use of my money right now. Get the idea?

When we make financial decisions with the big picture in mind and evaluate a variety of options with the help of a competent advisor to determine which one best fits our personal goals, we always can be confident that we made the best possible decision. We will be free from the anxiety that comes from other people telling us we made a mistake. We will not be subject to bias, hype, or the opinions of others.

Of course circumstances and goals change over time. Tax laws change. Markets fluctuate. These and other issues may cause us to alter our course every once in a while. However, we can still be satisfied that in the moment each decision was made, it was perfectly in line with our objectives at the time.

Throughout this book we will take an in-depth look at how the different areas of personal finance fit together and what is the proper order of priorities. Since everyone's resources are limited, no one is able to do everything they want to do at once. We must be sure to tackle the most critical areas first and then patiently build over time. My hope is that this book will improve your ability to maintain financial security throughout your entire life, no matter what unexpected events may threaten to throw you off track. Enjoy!

1

Which Road Will You Take?

"Two roads diverged in a yellow wood,
And sorry I could not travel both...
I took the one less traveled by,
And that has made all the difference."

(Excerpt from "The Road Not Taken" by Robert Frost)

The Choice Is Yours

One of life's greatest gifts is that we are free to choose how we spend our money, time, and other resources. However, we cannot control the consequences of our choices. The financial decisions we make over time will ultimately lead us to a certain destination, which may or may not be what we originally had in mind.

If I need to get to a meeting in Los Angeles that starts five hours from now, I must immediately start driving south on the freeway from where I live in Las Vegas. If I choose the northbound on-ramp instead and do not realize my mistake for a while, I will be late for my appointment. If I never realize my mistake, eventually I will end up in Salt Lake City, regardless of where I originally intended to go.

Money decisions work the same way. We must decide where we want to go and find out which road will get us there. Some financial roads may lead to greater freedom, such as the flexibility to work fewer hours or take more vacations. Others may severely limit future choices.

Without realizing it, this very moment many people are choosing a road that will never allow them to retire with the lifestyle they have come to expect. Some people are choosing a road that eventually leads to bankruptcy, while others are choosing a road that will lead to a lifetime of freedom and abundance.

At times we may not realize we are on the wrong path until it is too late to go back. We must constantly pay attention to which direction each financial decision is leading us and seek guidance from those who know the right way to the destination we seek. Although others can lead and coax us, we each must take full responsibility for our own decisions and select our path wisely.

Opportunity Costs

Every time we buy something, we give up the opportunity to use that money for something else. Economists call this "opportunity cost." If I buy a new car for $40,000, I can no longer invest that money. If I had invested the $40,000 and earned 5% tax-free interest for 30 years, that money could have grown to almost $173,000. So what is the real cost of my new car, $40,000 or $173,000?

Alternatively, I could have spent the $40,000 on several incredible family vacations, which might have created unique educational opportunities for my children, a stronger family bond, and fond memories to cherish for life. Which of these three choices is best—a new car, investing the money, or the vacations?

Sometimes the opportunity cost of a financial decision is even more meaningfully weighed in non-monetary terms. Buying things we cannot really afford may result in less time with family, working several years longer than we originally intended to work, or many sleepless nights.

Finite Resources

Even the richest people on the planet are faced with these either/or financial decisions because money is finite. No one ever has enough money to do everything they want, no matter how much they have. We cannot take both roads, as Robert Frost points out. Every financial decision we make is mutually exclusive.

Spending money is not bad. That is its ultimate purpose. We just need to be aware of the true cost of every spending decision if we want to be financially secure. We must be sure we are not trading what we want *most* for what we want *now*. As we develop a greater awareness of the true costs of our financial decisions, we become empowered to resist the urge to splurge. We realize that the costs of overspending often far outweigh the benefits. Every time we want to buy something, we should ask ourselves whether the purchase will move us towards fulfilling our greatest desires, or away from them.

What Do You Want Most in Life?

Everyone has a unique perspective on life. When first meeting with an advisor, you should share as much as possible about your personal goals and concerns so his recommendations will be consistent with *your* desires. You must clearly articulate what you want most so you can use your priorities as a measuring stick. If you don't know what you want, how can you effectively decide what to do?

Lewis Carroll masterfully captured this concept in *Alice's Adventures in Wonderland*, in which Alice asks the Cheshire Cat, "Would you tell me, please, which way I ought to go from here?"

"That depends a good deal on where you want to get to," said the Cat.

"I don't much care where--" said Alice.

"Then it doesn't matter which way you go," said the Cat.

Here are some examples of what I have articulated as my biggest priorities in life:

1. To be at peace with God, other people, and myself.
2. To have great relationships with my wife, children, extended family and friends (in that order).

3. To help improve the lives of other people as much as possible through my profession and through community and church service.
4. To live a long, healthy, fun life!

On the surface, it may appear that these objectives have nothing to do with financial decisions, but they are actually very closely linked. For example, to be at peace with God, other people, and myself, I must be honest in all of my financial dealings. This means that I do not borrow more money than I know I can repay, I pay my bills on time, and I would rather starve than earn a living dishonestly. I strive to maintain a great relationship with my family by choosing a more conservative lifestyle that does not require me to work 80 hours a week. That way I can spend plenty of time with them and take time off when necessary to attend important family events. I also involve them in purchasing decisions to be sure that I am not sacrificing their wants or needs for what I want to buy.

Some of my personal financial decisions have helped me fulfill these priorities, but others have not. Obviously these are very general goals that are hard to quantify, but I still like to measure my decisions against these to be sure they are always consistent with my primary objectives. After you know your main goals, you can break them down into more specific components that support your main objectives.

Whatever your greatest priorities may be, my purpose is to help you make wise financial decisions so you will be able to attain them. On the next page you will have the opportunity to brainstorm about what you want most. After you have created a list, organize the items in order of importance.

List Your Greatest Priorities

List your greatest priorities here, in no particular order. You are just brainstorming:

Now list them in order of importance:

1.

2.

3.

4.

5.

6.

7.

8.

Devastating Results of Poor Financial Choices

It takes time and effort to decide what our biggest priorities are. It takes even more time and effort to be sure that our financial decisions are always in harmony with these priorities. However, the reward is well worth the price.

What is the alternative? Let me share with you some of the consequences I have seen people suffer as a result of poor financial decisions that were inconsistent with what they really wanted most:

- Constant stress and worry
- Nervousness
- Sleepless nights
- Obsessive preoccupation with money, with difficulty focusing on other things
- Fear of losing money or other possessions
- Taking too much risk with investments
- Missing out on investment growth opportunities
- Obsession over daily market fluctuations
- Poor physical health
- Poor mental, emotional, and spiritual health
- Strained family relationships
- Divorce
- Lack of freedom to change jobs or start a new business
- Lack of freedom to move to a new location
- Having to move in with extended family members
- Delayed retirement
- Inability to retire *ever*
- Inability to help others in need
- Poor performance at work
- Job loss
- Inability to appreciate the simple beauties of life
- Inability to obtain a quality education
- Inability to help provide a quality education for children or grandchildren
- Lack of passion, ambition, and excitement for life

- Lack of trust in others
- Lack of trust by others
- Indecisiveness stemming from fear of making another mistake
- Procrastination
- Overeating
- Oversleeping
- Shoddy personal appearance
- Loss of creativity
- Loss of self esteem
- Hopelessness
- Alcohol, tobacco, and drug abuse
- Suicide

What is the cost of making casual financial decisions which are inconsistent with our biggest goals in life? Do you really believe that one poor financial decision could directly cause a number of these undesirable results?

Have you experienced any of these conditions yourself? If so, can you trace any of them back to a particular financial decision? If you think about it, one serious financial mistake in an extreme case could actually cause *all* of the maladies listed above.

Benefits of Wise Financial Choices

Perhaps the greatest value anyone could receive from working with a financial advisor is what I call "Big Mistake Insurance." This means that when an advisor helps to ensure that all financial decisions are consistent with your most important priorities, you can avoid many, if not all, of the symptoms listed above. Contrast the list above with the following results I have observed in many people who have clearly defined what they want most and have generally made wise financial decisions consistent with those priorities:

- Security
- Confidence
- Peace of mind
- Ability to sleep well at night
- Ability to wake up early, excited for the start of each new day
- Feeling of control over life and material things
- Reduced stress
- Greater ability to focus on other things besides money
- General detachment from material possessions
- Emotional detachment from short-term market performance
- Healthy, consistent returns on investments
- Great physical health
- Great mental, emotional, and spiritual health
- Loving family relationships
- Strong marriage
- Freedom to change jobs or start a new business
- Freedom to move to a new location
- Secure retirement
- Ability to help others in need
- Excellent performance at work
- Ability to appreciate the simple beauties of life
- Ability to obtain a quality education
- Ability to help provide a quality education for children or grandchildren
- Passion, ambition, and excitement for life
- Ability to easily trust others
- Trusted easily by others
- Ability to make quick and firm decisions
- Healthy, vibrant appearance
- Increased creativity
- High self esteem
- Ability to travel, shop, golf, boat, ski, and generally live a full, fun life!

How does that sound? Is it worth exercising a little self-discipline and sacrificing some of what you want *now* to obtain what you want *most* in life?

The choice is yours. Which road will you take?

2

Money Is a Curious Thing

What Is Money?

Sometimes we get so caught up in the day-to-day use of money and become so obsessed with acquiring more of it that we fail to see it for what it really is. Therefore, let's fundamentally define "money" and contemplate its role in our lives.

Money is simply a medium of exchange. It means nothing until it is converted into something else—any product or service that money can buy. Without money we would be forced to obtain goods and services from each other through a barter system. This would be a nightmare because our every want would have to be provided by someone who also wants exactly what we can provide. Despite its many faults, our modern financial system allows for an incredibly efficient exchange of value throughout the world, enabling us to enjoy a much higher quality of life than we ever could through a barter system.

Why Do We Want Money?

Since we do not operate under a barter system, we need money to function. The more we have, the more we can partake of all the wonderful things this bountiful world has to offer. However, we must be careful not to become too obsessed with acquiring more and more of it, because no matter how much we have, we can never fully satisfy our wants. If we are not careful, an infatuation with the pursuit of money can destroy us. Benjamin Franklin observed, "Money never made a man happy yet, nor will it. There is nothing in its nature to produce happiness. The more a man has, the more he wants. Instead of its filling a vacuum, it makes one."

Some people become so obsessed with acquiring more money that they forget what it is really for. It becomes a symbol of power or a game to see how much they can amass, even if they already have far more than they ever intend to spend in their lifetime. Rather than using money as a means to an end, the acquisition of money becomes the end objective. They may erroneously believe that having tons of money will solve all of their problems and bring them great happiness. They may think that great wealth will erase their fear because it will grant them security. Ironically, I have seen in many cases that great wealth often has the opposite effect because the more people have, the more they fear losing it.

As a society, why do we have such a tendency to hoard money? Could it be generated by the fear of not having enough, not knowing when we will be able to get more, or the desire for a life of ease? Of course we need to set aside and protect a certain amount of money for a rainy day and for the twilight of our lives when we may no longer be able to work. However, once we have enough to meet our basic needs, what are we giving up to incessantly pile up more? How much more good could we be doing with our money, time, and abilities to benefit other people if we were not hoarding it all for ourselves?

It has been interesting to observe the general lack of regard for money among my children, whose ages currently range from three to eight years. Sometimes when we give them cash they leave it lying around rather than carefully guarding it and tracking it as most adults would. Often it disappears among their mounds of toys or behind dressers. We exclaim, "Take care of your money! Don't you want to hang onto it so you can buy something fun with it later?" I am surprised at how long they are taking to appreciate its value and to be interested in wanting more of it.

Perhaps my children's indifference towards money stems from the fact that all of their needs and many of their wants have always been provided for them automatically. Maybe people cannot really value money until they have to work for it, or until they know how it feels to not have enough of it to meet even their most basic needs. Maybe the people who hoard money the most are the people who have felt most strongly the pains of poverty.

Although my children certainly need to develop a greater respect for money, can we learn something from them about not being so attached to it? I am touched by their confidence that their needs will always be met and by their satisfaction for what they already have. I never hear them talk about wanting a bigger house or a nicer car, or wishing that we would take more vacations.

How Do We Get Money?

Warren Buffet, one of the richest people in the world, said there are only two ways to make money: find value or create value. There is no such thing as something for nothing.

This morning at the gym I overheard a middle-aged man talking to the man next to him. He just found out that an old girlfriend of his from many years back recently inherited $130 million, so he is planning to call her. He said, "Hopefully she still loves me." I am amazed that so many people are always searching for a quick path to easy money.

Too many people think society owes them a living. Of course we all have an obligation to care for those who truly are physically or mentally unable to care for themselves. Extenuating circumstances may also necessitate a temporary lending hand even to capable people. Otherwise, everyone who is physically and mentally able to earn their own living must accept their responsibility to do so, no matter how difficult it might be. Those who do so feel much better about themselves and become a benefit to society rather than a burden.

We should never seek to take money away from others without giving adequate value in return. This is one of the reasons I am not a fan of gambling. In order for one party to win, all other parties involved must lose.

There are many ways we can acquire money legitimately through finding value or creating value. We can find value by purchasing property that generates current income, that has the potential to generate income in the future, or that we hope to be able to sell at a future date for more than what we paid for it. We can create value by inventing something useful, building something helpful, or rendering valuable personal service.

Those of us who are self-employed or own a business create value by providing products or services the public wants. We are paid by our customers for delivering that value. The amount of income we can generate is determined by the quality, quantity, and spirit of the service we give.

Those of us who are employees create value by providing services our employer needs to effectively deliver their products or services to the public. Sometimes I hear employees complain that all they are doing is working hard to make someone else rich. If that is true, what is wrong with that? An employer will only hire me if she believes that she will make more money after paying me than she could make without me.

Complaining does not solve anything. Those who are not satisfied with their current income should seek to create more value for their employer through increased education or stronger work ethic, find another employer who values their contribution more, or try their hand at delivering products or services directly to the public. Unfortunately, after going out on their own to spite their employer, some people discover that they were actually taking home a lot more money as employees than they ended up being able to make on their own. Working to increase the wealth of an employer is not demeaning as long as we are being fairly compensated for the value we create for the employer.

Is Money Good or Bad?

The Bible is often misquoted as stating that money is the root of all evil. Not so. The Bible actually states that "the *love* of money is the root of all evil" (1 Timothy 6:10, emphasis added). That is a very important distinction.

Money is not inherently bad. In fact, great good can be done with money when it is used properly. Good people are often empowered to do even more good when they have money. Think of the Good Samaritan in the Bible. If he were penniless, his ability to care for the man who had been mugged would have been severely diminished, because he would not have been able to pay the inn keeper (see Luke 10:25-37). Thousands of charitable organizations which do a tremendous amount of good throughout the world could not exist without the generous donations of many affluent people.

On the other hand, when we set our hearts upon our possessions, hoard them all for ourselves, or covet other people's riches, we are headed down a dangerous road that will certainly lead to misery. We must learn to love people, not money. When we truly love God and other people, and demonstrate our love through our generosity, God will be more willing to help us obtain money because he knows we will use it for the right purposes.

What Should We Do with Our Money?

Obviously, the primary purpose of money is to provide for the basic necessities of life: food, clothing, and shelter. After we have met these three basic needs, the choices for what to do with our surplus are endless.

I believe that someday we will be accountable to God for how profitably we utilized our resources throughout our lives. Everything we have comes from the great Creator of the universe. When we die, we cannot take any of it with us, so is it really ours to keep? No, we are just stewards over our material possessions for the short time we live on earth, then they will be passed on to someone else.

The rewards we receive throughout life and after we die will be based on how wisely we utilize the money, time, and talents we are granted. It does not matter how much or how little we have. All that matters is whether we were good stewards over what we were given and how effectively we used it to benefit others. Even if you do not believe in a supreme being, you must admit that you feel best about yourself when you know you are

using your resources to their greatest advantage and not just for
your own benefit.

What Is a Good Steward?

I love the description the Lord gave of a good steward in his
"Parable of the Talents" (see Matthew 25:14-30). In this parable,
a man gave each of his three servants stewardship over a portion
of his money while he was travelling to a distant land. He gave
five talents to one, two to another, and one to the last, based on
each servant's ability. A talent was a sum of money.

While he was away, the first servant wisely invested the five
talents he was given and earned an additional five talents. Simi-
larly, the servant with two talents earned another two talents. The
last servant was afraid of losing the one talent he was given, so
he just buried it in the ground.

When the master returned, he asked for a report. He was very
pleased with the first two servants because they both had doubled
the value of what they had been given. Hence, he gave them both
the same reward: "Well done, thou good and faithful servant:
thou hast been faithful over a few things, I will make thee ruler
over many things: enter thou into the joy of thy lord" (Matthew
25:21).

However, the master was angry with the last servant for being lazy and not making good use of what he had been given. He
took the talent he had been given and gave it to the servant with
ten talents. Then he ordered, "…cast ye the unprofitable servant
into outer darkness: there shall be weeping and gnashing of
teeth" (Matthew 25:30).

I find it fascinating that he who turned two talents into four
received the same reward as he who turned five talents into ten.
Even though the servant with two talents did not earn as much,
he was considered to be just as profitable because he also ob-
tained a 100% return. This was just a test to see how wisely each
servant would manage a small stewardship so the master could
determine whether they would be worthy of receiving much
more.

It appears that the unprofitable servant who had received only one talent might have received the same reward as the other two if he had been able to obtain just one talent more than what he received. I am struck by the harshness of his punishment for not doing so. What can we learn from this? Is God testing us the same way right now?

The size of our annual income does not matter as much as how wisely we use what we receive. I have met people earning $100,000 per year who are millionaires because they have always lived well below their means, saved a large percentage of their income, and invested wisely. On the other hand, I have met people earning $1,000,000 per year who are just a step away from bankruptcy because they have always spent almost everything they make, incurred huge amounts of debt, and invested mainly in very risky assets, if at all.

Of course I am not suggesting that this parable is only about investing, because it certainly also applies to the proper use of our gifts, abilities, time, knowledge, and other resources, as well as how well we use our money to improve the lives of other people. Surely someone who earns $100,000 a year and gives 10% of it away to people in need will be viewed much more favorably in the eyes of God than someone making $1,000,000 a year who wisely invests 50% of it but gives nothing to others.

Furthermore, I am not suggesting that all of our extra money after meeting basic needs should be invested or given to other people. Sometimes spending money on wholesome recreational activities or for our children's education is more important. The point is that we need to exercise a balanced approach as we carefully consider what the best use of our money might be in each circumstance. If we are good stewards, we will always treat money with great respect, rather than buying whatever we want, whenever we want it, regardless of the consequences.

Why Is It So Hard to Make and Keep Money?

Many people struggle to make enough money to meet their financial obligations. Many people also find it incredibly difficult to stick to a budget. Why is this? It is just simple math, right? Is it really that hard to add and subtract?

If successful money management were as simple as being able to add, subtract, multiply and divide numbers, everyone who could perform these basic calculations would be financially secure. Unfortunately, financial problems stem from much more complex issues than math problems. They are rooted in psychological and behavioral deficiencies, such as lack of work ethic, lack of faith, lack of discipline, over-spending, excessive risk-taking in investments, greed, pride, and an insatiable desire to impress others.

These issues are common to the human race and are much more difficult to master than math problems. My hope is that as we address these deficiencies throughout this book, you will recognize which ones you suffer from so you can be more fully empowered to overcome them.

What Is the Biggest Threat to Financial Security?

Of all the psychological and behavioral deficiencies mentioned above, one especially curious phenomenon deeply impacts the financial decisions we make. We are all affected by it. No one is immune to it, including myself. It is commonly known as "keeping up with the Joneses."

We enter dangerous ground when we care more about what others think of us than we care about doing what is right for ourselves and our families. This is a slippery slope that can ruin us financially because we can never be completely satisfied that we are impressing everyone around us. We will always be able to find someone who has more and better things than we do.

The sad news is that even if we spend every last penny to impress others, most of the people we are trying to impress may never even notice. Most people do not care about our image as much as we think they do. Think about it. How much time do *you* spend thinking about how idiotic someone is because they drive a junky old car or how awesome another person is because they live in a mansion? If you notice at all, I suspect you may give it a fleeting thought for a few seconds, and then you move on to focus on what you are trying to accomplish.

No one is really paying much attention to our possessions. They are all too busy worrying about themselves. If we do have friends who make fun of us for not buying all the expensive toys they have, maybe we shouldn't hang out with them so much. Many reckless spenders poke at frugal people because deep down they envy their stronger financial position. They put others down to elevate themselves and to justify their own wasteful splurges.

I have been practicing financial planning long enough to realize that many, if not most, of the people who flaunt an aura of success actually have very little wealth and a lot of debt. Those who can see the truth behind the façade are not so envious of their glamorous image because they know that it comes at a hefty price, often in the form of high stress, depression, failed marriages, or poor health.

I also have observed that many of those who appear to be poor are actually the ones with all the money, no debt, and much less stress. They figured out a long time ago that they did not want to be like the Joneses at all.

Many years ago I met a young couple who lived a very nice lifestyle spending more each month than they were making. They had a sizeable mountain of debt, no savings, and very little insurance. They said, "We just realized the other day that we have already accomplished all of our goals in life and we are not even thirty yet. We have the home of our dreams, a pool, a boat, and our dream cars. What do we do now?"

I was dumbfounded by their perspective and thought to myself, "How about starting to pay for it!" Unfortunately, within a year the husband was seriously injured so he was not able to work for a while, then his company let him go when the economy turned south. Needless to say, they lost everything—or at least that is what they would tell you. In reality, they did not really lose anything, except maybe their pride and their credit, because none of it was legitimately theirs to begin with. They were only living an illusion of wealth. They are the Joneses that we are all trying to keep up with.

The temptation to "keep up with the Joneses" may be the single biggest threat to our financial security, both now and in the future. It stems from one of the most common and powerful fears from which people suffer: the fear of criticism. If we can overcome the fear of criticism, we will be well on our way to overcoming this tendency. To borrow from the wisdom of Benjamin Franklin again, "The eyes of other people are the eyes that ruin us. If all but myself were blind, I should want neither fine clothes, fine houses, nor fine furniture."

When we live joyfully within our means without worrying about what other people have or what other people think of us, we break free from being slaves to our possessions and income. This freedom allows us to pursue meaningful work that we enjoy, where we can make the biggest possible difference for good in the world.

By living modestly, we also set a conservative standard for our children and grandchildren that may give them greater freedom to pursue their dreams. Otherwise, they might feel pressured to take a high-paying job that they hate, just to support an extravagant lifestyle they were raised to expect.

How many people are trying to keep up with us although we are totally unaware of it? By living well below our means, we may be granting permission to others to do the same by placing less pressure on them to keep up with us.

As we pursue the acquisition of money, let us always remember what it is really for so we will maintain proper balance in our lives and use it for the greatest possible good.

3

Channel the Flow to Make Things Grow

A Lesson from Farming

When I was just out of high school, a wise church leader gave a small group of us some much-needed financial counsel that I will never forget. All of us were about to leave home and become responsible for our own money management for the first time, so he wanted to be sure we would use our money wisely.

He grew up on a farm in a small town in Idaho where they only had the opportunity to water their crops once a day for a limited time. There was an irrigation canal that flowed past their farm, and at a specific pre-appointed time they were allowed to open the flood gate leading to their farm. They set up a system of dikes and ditches so the water would naturally flow to all of their crops.

They had to constantly maintain these dikes and ditches to be sure they were prepared before the water came because the water would always take the path of least resistance. His father taught him, "We must channel the flow to make things grow."

It took a lot of discipline and hard work to be sure that the water went to the right places every day. On the days they were not as vigilant, some crops would not receive the amount of water needed. Once this water was lost, they could never get it back. Some crops died because they did not receive enough water, which resulted in lower yields at harvest time and lower income for their family.

This caring leader taught us that money works the same way. It always takes the path of least resistance, so we must be prepared with a specific plan for where we want the money to go before we receive it. Then we can be sure it will go to the best use. We must set up barriers for ourselves—rules for what we will not spend money on so it will not be wasted. We must "channel the flow to make things grow."

Channel Your Cash Flow

Have you noticed that whenever we receive money, it somehow always seems to magically flow through our fingers like sand flowing through an hourglass? It is very difficult to hang onto. Perhaps this is why in the financial services industry we call it "cash flow."

Most people put much less thought into where their money is going than into what they will do this weekend or where they will go on their next vacation. Then they wonder why they never seem to be able to get ahead financially. Before the money arrives, we must set up financial dikes and ditches—strict financial priorities, rules, and boundaries for ourselves—so our money will be used for the things that are most important to us. Yes, work is required, but the reward is well worth the effort.

Once we decide where we want our money to go, we need to make the flow as automatic as possible to be sure it consistently goes to the right places. I am a huge fan of direct deposits and automatic withdrawals, not only because they are less work, but also because they make the discipline of regular saving and investing much easier. It is psychologically much less painful than having to decide every month to write a check to a savings or investment account.

Properly channeling our cash flow is easier said than done. As mentioned in the last chapter, successful money management is not so much about math as it is about personal discipline, sacrifice, and having a clear vision of what we want to accomplish. It has much more to do with emotions and behavior than with numbers.

First Things First

The best way to ensure that the most important things are taken care of is to pay for those things first. We should pay our existing commitments fully and on time before we buy other things we want. We should be honest in all financial dealings with others, whether they are individuals or large institutions. The failure of many people to live by this principle is largely what caused the real estate market and stock market collapse in 2008-2009, which resulted in the biggest recession since the Great Depression.

How many times have you told yourself that at the end of the month you will throw whatever is left over into a savings account? Is any money ever left over? If you are like most people, this approach never results in much surplus because somehow we never quite have enough money to buy all the things we want.

Many years ago I met a man who was consistently making about $800,000 per year. All he had to show for it when I first met him was $200,000 in savings, a huge house, a few fancy cars, a bunch of toys, and millions of dollars worth of debt. He was frustrated because he felt like no matter how much money he made, he never had quite enough to buy everything he wanted. He complained that some of his buddies were making well over $1,000,000 a year, and was convinced that if he could just get his income up to that level, then he would be happy. He was generally a miserable, cynical person who hated his job and kept saying he couldn't wait to retire, yet wasn't doing much to prepare for it.

I realized in that moment that it really is not possible for anyone to ever make enough money to buy everything they could possibly want. That is why it doesn't work to save whatever is left over at the end of the month. If we really want to build savings or investments, we must make it one of our top priorities by doing so at the *beginning* of every month. Everything else will work itself out.

The IRS discovered this principle a long time ago. They require that our estimated taxes be withheld from every paycheck before we can spend it, or at least sent in on a quarterly basis for those who are self-employed. They know they would be much less likely to receive the full amount to which they are entitled if they depended on us to send them one big check on April 15 each year.

Have you noticed that it also happens to be less painful to pay our taxes this way? We tend not to feel the full cost of the taxes we pay when it comes out of our paycheck automatically before we even receive it. Have you ever had to pay extra when you filed your tax return because you were not having enough withheld? It hurts, doesn't it? How much worse would it hurt if we had to come up with the full amount every year on April 15? Why not use this principle to our own advantage by systematically saving a percentage of every paycheck before spending any of it?

Prudent Cash Flow Hierarchy

When it comes to money management, what should be our first priorities? Allocating our funds in the following order is critical to ensuring financial security throughout life:

1. Taxes
2. Tithing (charitable contributions)
3. Protection (insurance and legal documents)
4. Asset Building (savings and investments)
5. Current Lifestyle (everything else)

Taxes

Although it pains me to list this as the first priority, above all else I believe in obeying the law and in paying all obligations fully and on time. I have met too many self-employed people who severely underestimated the amount of taxes that would be due at the end of a very profitable year. Many of these could not come up with enough cash to foot the bill in time because they had already spent their money on other things.

We should always have an adequate amount withheld from our paychecks or keep more than enough set aside to pay our taxes before allocating funds to other categories. If we fall short when taxes are due, we may get hit with huge penalties, interest charges, and maybe even jail time, all of which can diminish our financial security. Of course we want to look for legitimate ways to reduce taxes as much as possible, but we all must pay our fair share.

Tithing

Everything we have comes from God, so in reality giving back at least 10% of what we make is a very small sacrifice, if even a sacrifice at all. The more we give, the more we receive, either in temporal or spiritual benefits. In ancient times, people would give the "firstlings of the flock" and the "first fruits of the field" to demonstrate their absolute commitment to God and their willingness to give. Today we can demonstrate the same attitude by giving 10% of our income as soon as we receive it before spending it on anything else.

Tithing our income helps us keep things in proper perspective, be more grateful for what we have, utilize our resources more wisely, and become less emotionally attached to our wealth. We also find deeper satisfaction in life knowing that we are contributing to a good cause and helping others in need.

God has not promised that we will be rich if we tithe our income, but he has promised that our needs will always be met and that we will receive great blessings, some of which may be of even greater value than monetary wealth. He said, "Bring ye all the tithes into the storehouse, that there may be meat in mine house, and prove me now herewith, saith the LORD of hosts, if I will not open you the windows of heaven, and pour you out a blessing, that there shall not be room enough to receive it" (Malachi 3:10).

I have witnessed so many of these promised blessings fulfilled in my own life and in the lives of other people that I am afraid to stop tithing my income because I do not want to lose the blessings! How can we expect God to help us if we fail to do as he asks?

Also keep in mind that those who give the most throughout their lives, monetarily and otherwise, find that in their times of greatest need they are surrounded by family and friends who are willing to give in return. The more willingly and quietly we give, without complaining or seeking credit, the more we will benefit from giving.

Even if you are not religious, you must at least acknowledge that most of who you are and what you have been able to accomplish is a product of the impact that countless other people have had on you: your spouse, parents, grandparents, siblings, children, aunts, uncles, teachers, coaches, friends, neighbors, employers, and co-workers, as well as others who you may never meet, such as government leaders, authors, and philosophers. It would be impossible to fully repay all of the people who have contributed to your success. You must pay it forward by helping others.

If you do not want to pay tithing to a religious organization, try giving at least 10% of your income to family or friends in need, or to some other charitable cause you believe is worthy of your support. You may be surprised to discover how great you will feel and how much better off you will be for having done so.

In the words of the Master Teacher, "It is more blessed to give than to receive" (Acts 20:35). Whether we donate 10% of our income to a religious organization or make other charitable contributions, this must be a top priority, even before paying ourselves.

Protection

Would you buy a Lamborghini if you did not have a secure garage to store it in? Would you dare drive it off the lot without first having an alarm installed? Would you ever buy a house without simultaneously purchasing a homeowners insurance policy in case it burned down the day you bought it, even if it were not required by a mortgage company?

Lamborghinis and houses are expensive purchases, so I doubt that very many people would purchase either one without first considering how to protect their investment through insurance and other means. Protection considerations take priority over asset building because without adequate protection, assets that took a lifetime to build could be wiped out in an instant. We will discuss this more in the next chapter.

Asset Building

Have you ever heard the phrase, "pay yourself first?" That is a very good rule of thumb after taxes, tithing, and protection considerations. "Pay yourself first" means we should save for future needs before buying the things we want now.

Most people find it very difficult to build significant assets because they do not have the discipline to sacrifice what they want now so they can have what they want most at some future date. They erroneously believe that they just need to get lucky with a risky investment or win the lottery to be wealthy.

Building wealth can be a relatively simple process. All we need to do is consistently save at least 20% of our income and invest it wisely. If we are not willing to do this, we may never be able to get ahead financially or retire with a decent standard of living. Although it is simple, it is not always easy. We will discuss this more in Chapter Six.

Current Lifestyle

Finally, we get to spend some money! If we can be disciplined enough to take care of all the preceding concerns first, then live within whatever is left, we will essentially be financially bullet-proof throughout life. When we know we are taking care of the other essential areas, spending money is more fun because we do not have to feel guilty or wonder whether we can really afford to spend it.

Most people are stressed out about money because they have it all backwards. They spend everything they make—or even more than what they make—to meet their current wants, then hope that nothing bad ever happens to them. They live paycheck-to-paycheck with very little flexibility. They view every little unexpected expense as a major crisis because they have no wiggle room.

Do you like to keep a budget? Most people I have met hate it with a passion and have a very hard time keeping one. If you fall into that category, I have good news for you. When you take care of your taxes, tithing, protection, and savings first, you no longer have to keep a budget. Just drain your account at the end of every month, but don't spend more than what is left in your account. Then repeat the process at the beginning of the next month.

Of course you may still benefit from keeping a more detailed budget, but if you find that you just cannot get it going, it is not absolutely necessary. If you abide by these cash flow rules, the important things will always be taken care of. We will discuss this more in Chapter Seven.

Avoid Debt like The Plague

In order to make this cash flow hierarchy work without having to budget everything we spend, we must have the discipline to stop spending when we run out of money for the month. Most of us are so driven by our desire to keep up with the Joneses and to have what we want now without regard to what it might cost us later that we readily go into debt for whatever we want.

We should treat the act of acquiring debt with grave seriousness. Although we tend to treat it casually, it is nothing short of self-imposed servitude that threatens our financial security, marriages, dreams, and sanity.

At one time The Plague was the most dreaded disease. Historians estimate that during the 14th century it wiped out at least 30% of the European population.[1] What percentage of Americans has been wiped out financially by the modern plague of excessive debt?

Avoiding debt is much easier than trying to get out of debt, just like avoiding that first cigarette is much easier than trying to quit smoking. Whenever we go into debt we are spending part of our future now without knowing whether we will be able to afford it later. Many successful people have lived by the motto, "If I can't buy it with cash, I can't afford it."

Reducing, eliminating, and avoiding debt are all critical to long-term financial security. High monthly payment obligations extending into our golden years may postpone or jeopardize our ability to retire. Interest charges can consume our potential to build wealth.

If I buy a new TV for $2,500 on a credit card charging 18% interest and always make only the minimum monthly payment, it would take me 28 years to pay it off, and my total cost would be $8,397 for a TV that would be long gone by then. A $300,000 30-year fixed mortgage at 6% interest ends up costing $647,509 over the course of 30 years.

We cannot make financial progress by paying 18% in credit card debt while earning 6% on our investments. In order to become financially secure, we must find a way to make interest work in our favor, not against us.

History of the Plastic Plague

Where did this modern epidemic of what I call the "Plastic Plague" come from? Most of us have been taught that buying things on credit is not only normal, but also the smartest way to purchase. We think we have to pay for everything with a credit card so we can rack up as many rewards points as possible and improve our credit score. We have been taught to maintain a mortgage even if we have enough money to pay it off so we can deduct the interest off of our taxes. Lending institutions have done a great job convincing us that what is in their best interest is also in our best interest.

What is the origin of our current society's attitudes towards debt? What did we do before car loans existed? Did you know that Henry Ford believed as a matter of principle that no one should ever buy a car on credit? He invented major break-throughs in production efficiency to drive costs down so his automobiles would be more affordable to the middle class, but he still expected everyone to pay cash.

No other manufacturer could quite compete with the very in-expensive Model T Ford until 1919 when General Motors formed its own lending institution, General Motors Acceptance Corporation (GMAC). This innovation allowed average people to buy GM's higher-priced, more luxurious automobiles with lower payments over time. By 1926 three-fourths of all car sales in America were financed.[2]

Sticking to his principles, Henry Ford fought this movement as long as possible, and thus suffered a dramatic decline in sales. In 1927 Ford Motor Company was finally forced to set up its own credit arm in order to compete.[3]

The U.S. Department of Housing and Urban Development states that before the Federal Housing Administration (FHA) was created in 1934, "mortgage loan terms were limited to 50 percent of the property's market value, with a repayment schedule spread over three to five years and ending with a balloon payment." This new government program was created to stimulate the slug-gish housing industry during the Great Depression by making home purchases feel more affordable. It dramatically reduced the amount required for down payment and allowed for lower monthly payments stretched out over much longer periods, such as 20 or 30 years, which we now think of as the norm.[4]

Can you believe that credit cards did not even exist until the 1950s? That is only about 60 years ago at the time of this writ-ing.[5] How did people survive for thousands of years before credit cards were introduced? Are they really as essential as we think they are?

Easy access to credit has allowed us to easily spend more than we make without realizing it until it is too late. Once we have tasted the sweet savor of getting what we want now without having to pay for it until later, it is very difficult to go back to paying cash for everything. That is why GM's idea exploded so rapidly, and that is why our society is so addicted to debt.

However, there can be severe consequences for being allured by tantalizing opportunities to buy now and pay later. Although it may feel good in the beginning, most of us are oblivious to the true costs of going into debt.

True Cost of Debt

When we take out a loan to buy something we cannot afford to buy with cash, we make it even more expensive over time by adding loan origination fees and interest charges. We are also likely to accept a larger initial purchase price and be fooled into thinking it is not very expensive because the payments feel small when stretched out over a long period of time.

Car dealers are trained to use this psychological phenomenon against us. I have been very frustrated with several car salesmen who would only answer in terms of a monthly payment whenever I asked about the purchase price of a car. They avoided discussing the full price because they thought they could charge me more by making it look like only a small monthly obligation, even if it meant extending the loan term.

When we pay cash up front, we more keenly feel the true cost of what we are buying. It hurts to let go of a big chunk of change that took a while to build up, so we tend to be more determined to find the lowest possible purchase price by shopping around and aggressively bargaining for a steep discount.

Someone I know who drove an old, beat-up car for years demonstrated this principle. He has no debt—not even a mortgage—and a lot of money in liquid savings and other investments. For a long time he said that he should probably buy a new car because his old one kept breaking down, but he simply did not want to part with any of his savings. He remarked, "It would be so easy to just pick up a car loan for $400 a month, which wouldn't feel like much, but I don't want to take on the burden of a monthly payment. I also know that a loan would end up costing me more in the long run than if I paid cash."

He finally replaced it with a newer used car, but shopped around to get the best deal he could find and paid cash for it so he is still debt-free. He continues to contribute to savings every month, so next time he needs to buy a new car he will have plenty of money to do so again without incurring interest charges. Although he was unemployed for a while during this period, he was easily able to weather the storm because he had no monthly debt payments to worry about and plenty of assets to cover his other modest expenses.

I am not suggesting that we should all drive around old, beat-up cars. Spending a lot of money on a nice car is fine if we can afford it. However, I think most people would spend a lot less on vehicles if they always paid cash rather than making small payments over time, even at 0% interest, because they would more acutely feel the true cost all at once.

What about credit card debt? When I buy a new house, shouldn't I furnish it right away with the amazing 0% interest offers I keep receiving in the mail? This may be an exciting proposition, but it is also a dangerous game because typically the 0% interest is offered only for the first 12-18 months. If we fail to pay off the entire balance by the end of the initial 0% period, interest will be due at a very high rate, typically at least 20%, starting from the original purchase date. In other words, if I charge $10,000 on this type of card and do not pay any of it back by the end of the initial 12-month interest-free period, my balance will suddenly jump to $12,000, and interest will continue to accrue at 20% or more from that point forward. If we cannot afford to pay cash for the furnishings when we first move into a new home, what makes us think we will be able to afford them 12 months later?

Another problem with purchasing everything on a credit card is that all the little purchases we do not track can eventually destroy us financially, just like a small unnoticeable water leak can cause severe structural damage over time. Even those who always pay off their entire balance each month to avoid interest charges are often flabbergasted when they review the report that details how much they spent in each category over the course of a year. I have met people who spend more eating out every night than they are saving for retirement without even realizing it because they were swiping it all on their credit card. At least they were getting points for their purchases so they could book free airline tickets and hotel rooms, which lead to even more over-spending!

Self-Imposed Slavery

Perhaps the most severe cost of going into debt is the resulting loss of freedom. It truly is a form of self-imposed slavery. Too few of us enjoy the level of freedom our founding fathers intended for us. We may not be oppressed by political dictators, but we often voluntarily submit ourselves to dictatorial creditors.

Many of us lock ourselves into huge long-term commitments without knowing whether our future circumstances will allow us to honor these obligations. We may barely be able to qualify for the payments on a large new home, but we want it so badly that we buy it anyway, in hopes that the payment will feel more affordable as our income goes up. Then the unthinkable happens: our income actually goes down, or stops completely, and we lose everything.

Consider the following observation by J. Reuben Clark, Jr: "Interest never sleeps nor sickens nor dies; it never goes to the hospital; it works on Sundays and holidays; it never takes a vacation; it never visits nor travels; it takes no pleasure; ...it has no love, no sympathy; it is as hard and soulless as a granite cliff. Once in debt, interest is your companion every minute of the day and night; you cannot shun it or slip away from it; you cannot dismiss it; it yields neither to entreaties, demands, or orders; and whenever you get in its way or cross its course or fail to meet its demands, it crushes you."[6]

Maybe part of the reason so many people readily incur excessive amounts of debt is that the penalty today for failing to meet our obligations is not very harsh. If we can no longer make our payments or just do not feel like making them anymore, we can simply walk away with a mere slap on the hand in the form of bad credit for a few years, and then begin the whole cycle all over again.

In Colonial America, people were much more hesitant to go into debt because declaring bankruptcy often resulted in literally becoming a slave to creditors, being imprisoned for life, having an ear cut off, or having a thumb branded with a "T" for "Thief." Of course I am not recommending a return to such barbaric practices. However, I do believe that we should treat debt with more seriousness than we do now.

Debt's power to diminish our liberty and happiness is demonstrated by the choices of a very successful businessman who a friend of mine was recently telling me about. He lives a very extravagant lifestyle but hates his job and dreams of becoming a high school basketball coach. When my friend suggested that he go for it, he said he could never make the switch because his monthly debt obligations are way too high, and he could never downsize because of the lifestyle his wife and children have come to expect. He has voluntarily locked himself out of opportunities to do what he loves doing most and has resigned to working very long, grueling hours at a job he hates for the rest of his career.

Conversely, another successful businessman I know has paid cash for almost everything he has bought all along the way. Although he may have been able to live an even nicer lifestyle if he had borrowed more, he lives very well. He has built a large, beautiful custom home with a very small mortgage payment. He drives high-end luxury vehicles, owns two fully furnished vacation properties, an RV, a boat, several four-wheelers, and travels a lot. Over the past couple of years the business he owns has taken a nose dive, like many other businesses, but he is one of the few I know in his situation who has been able to maintain all of his possessions because he does not owe anything to anyone, other than the small mortgage on his home. Of course he has cut back on many things he used to spend money on, but he is in a remarkably secure and flexible position compared to most of the people I know who enjoy a similar standard of living.

Although paying cash for everything requires sacrifice, humility, and patience, it is the safest, happiest way to pay for things because then we never risk buying something we cannot afford. Not owing anything to anyone is a great feeling.

I have been reading a bit of *Little House on the Prairie* to our children every night for the past couple of weeks, and one chapter really struck me the other night. In this part of the story, Pa was building a cabin out on the unsettled Kansas prairie without any nails because it was a very long trip to the nearest town. While chopping down trees for the cabin, he met another settler who lived several miles away. This man insisted that Pa borrow some nails from him to build a roof for the cabin. When Ma heard about it, she complained, "But I don't like to be beholden, not even to the best of neighbors." Pa responded, "Nor I. I've never been beholden to any man yet, and I never will be. But neighborliness is another matter, and I'll pay him back every nail as soon as I can make the trip to Independence."[7]

I thought to myself, "Wow, Ma would rather have Pa build a roof without nails than owe anyone anything!" I was also impressed with Pa's resolve to repay every single nail as soon as possible. What would our society be like today if everyone had the same attitude as the Ingalls family did then?

No matter how poor our spending decisions may have been in the past, we all have the power to change. We may not be able to regain our freedom from bondage overnight, but if we work hard and consistently spend less than we earn, we will inevitably emerge victorious over the chains of debt. When that glorious day arrives, we will realize that the reward is well worth the effort.

What we do with the money we receive drives everything else in our lives. Living by the cash flow hierarchy we discussed earlier and then living joyfully within whatever is left over is a vital step in our quest for financial security. Our future is filled with hope if we can truly learn to always "channel the flow to make things grow."

4

Expect the Best and Prepare for the Worst

Optimism vs. Naiveté

I am a very optimistic person. I feel strongly that if we expect good things to happen, they are much more likely to happen, and we will more easily recognize all the good things happening around us. If we constantly worry and focus too much on the negative, misfortune is more likely to come our way, and when it does come, we will magnify its impact through our pessimism. Even if the troubles that we fear never arrive, a negative attitude is a debilitating virus that impedes our productivity and enjoyment of life.

Still, we do not have complete control over our health, Mother Nature, or the potentially harmful actions of other people. Life is risky. Bad things happen, even in the face of the most positive attitude. Although optimism may improve our chances of a positive outcome, it cannot fully protect us from the reality of occasional disaster. Therefore, I echo Zig Ziglar's motto: "Expect the best. Prepare for the worst."

The Bible says, "Pride goeth before destruction, and an haughty spirit before a fall" (Proverbs 16:18). Ironically, the times that we feel most invincible may be the times that we are actually most susceptible to loss because we think that prudent precautions are no longer necessary. We must always be humble enough to acknowledge our own vulnerability. Only then will we take the steps necessary to strengthen our protection against the threats that surround us, thus truly becoming more invincible.

The tragic sinking of the Titanic on April 15, 1912 is a classic example of this principle. It was designed to be the largest, most luxurious, fastest, and safest ocean liner of its time. It was advertised as being unsinkable because of a new design boasting sixteen separate watertight compartments.

Since it was deemed unsinkable, it carried only the minimum required number of lifeboats, so as to maximize the amount of deck space available for first-class passengers. Thus only 705 of its 2228 passengers survived its maiden voyage from England to New York.

Despite receiving at least six warnings from other ships that there were icebergs ahead, Captain Edward John Smith maintained very high speeds in an effort to make headlines for arriving at New York in record time. In addition, the crow's nest was not equipped with binoculars as it normally should have been. Binoculars might have helped the crew detect the iceberg in time to avoid it.

Of course other factors contributed to the sinking of the Titanic, such as faulty ship construction and weather conditions. However, if Captain Smith had not considered the Titanic to be unsinkable, might he have protected the lives of all 2228 passengers, including his own, by traveling at a safer speed, ensuring the crow's nest was properly equipped with binoculars, and carrying enough lifeboats for everyone?

We must meet protection needs before considering how much to save and invest. Ignoring protection needs to build assets more quickly or to better keep up with the Joneses could result in devastating consequences, as we have learned from the Titanic. Without adequate protection in place, assets that took a lifetime to build could vanish in an instant, regardless of how optimistic we might feel. Doing everything we can to protect what we have provides a much stronger foundation for building wealth and gives us greater freedom not to worry about bad things that could happen.

What's the Plan?

Most of us skate through life without too many major catastrophes throwing us off track, so we tend to believe that none of the bad things that happen to other people will ever happen to us.

Hopefully they never will. The question is if they do happen to us, what will be the impact, and how will we deal with it?

If we are serious about maintaining financial security throughout our entire lives, we cannot just hope that nothing bad will ever occur. We must have a solid plan for how we would deal with any major catastrophe.

Some people say they have faith that God will always take care of them when trouble comes, so they do not need to plan. I agree that having complete trust in God is critical. Everything we have comes from him. However, faith does not absolve us of personal responsibility.

I have often noticed that God seems to be more willing to help those who have already done everything they can do for themselves. If we were to obtain whatever we desire merely by asking God for it, we would be robbed of the personal growth he wants us to acquire through our own efforts. He honors our free-dom of choice, even when our choices may cause severe injury to ourselves and others. True faith and hope are principles of ac-tion, not passive wishful dreams. We demonstrate our faith that we will always be okay by being reasonably prepared for the worst.

When we take the time to honestly assess the potential threats to our financial security and consciously decide how to address those threats, we feel greater peace of mind knowing that we will always be okay no matter what happens. Taking a methodical approach to risk analysis is important because we have the ten-dency to overestimate low-probability risks, such as the overthrow of the U.S. monetary system, and under-estimate higher-probability risks, such as the inability to work for an ex-tended period due to long-term illness or injury.

A qualified financial planner can help to accurately assess the true threats to financial security and plan out the most sensible approach to each one. Those who take this disciplined approach become more fearless, free to expect the best from life, because they know that they will be able to maintain financial security regardless of what surprises life throws at them.

What's your plan?

Four Ways to Manage Risk

Every risk we face can be addressed in one of four ways. Each may be an appropriate choice, depending on the circumstances and type of risk in question:

1. Avoidance
2. Reduction
3. Transfer
4. Retention

1. Avoiding Risk

The surest way to prevent the potential loss arising from a certain activity is to completely avoid it. For example, if I want to avoid the possibility of having to pay for a stranger's medical expenses due to an auto accident, I could stop driving a car. So why not just avoid all risks? The problem is that whenever we avoid a risk we also miss out on the benefits we could have received for participating in the associated activity. In addition, not all risks can be completely avoided, such as the risks of illness or natural disaster.

Avoidance may be appropriate for a limited number of risks that produce a high probability of loss, such as gambling, but it is not a practical solution for most risks. In some cases we may even create additional risks by trying to avoid a particular risk. For example, we may be tempted to keep all of our savings in cash to avoid the risk of investment losses, but then we would be subjecting ourselves to the potential risk of loss by inflation, which is practically guaranteed to significantly erode the value of our cash over time.

2. Reducing Risk

If we are unable or unwilling to avoid an activity, we can take steps to reduce the probability and potential severity of loss associated with the activity. For example, when we choose to drive, we can reduce the risk of being involved in an automobile accident by observing the speed limit and other traffic laws, not texting while driving, and not driving while drowsy or drunk. We can also reduce the severity of injury to ourselves in the case of an accident by always wearing our seatbelts and by driving vehicles with airbags. Other common examples of risk reduction include installing burglar and fire alarms, building locked fences around pools, and visiting the doctor once a year for a physical exam. When investing, we can reduce risk through proper due diligence, diversification, seeking the advice of qualified experts, and investing primarily in that which we understand or can control to some extent.

3. Transferring Risk

Another way to deal with risks we are unable or unwilling to completely avoid is to transfer them to a third party. We can transfer risk in several ways, but the most practical, cost-effective, and common approach for high-severity risks with a low probability of occurrence is through insurance. The most effective use of insurance is to cover only the unlikely potential losses which would financially devastate us if they occurred. In these areas, we should seek to maximize our protection and minimize the cost.

Life insurance is one example of appropriate risk transfer. If a young breadwinner with a non-working spouse and small children were to pass away prematurely, his or her family would find themselves in a very desperate financial situation. A young family is not likely to have enough assets to care for its own long-term needs without the breadwinner's earned income. Without adequate life insurance, the burden of providing for such a family may fall upon extended family, friends, church, or community.

After carefully considering the full potential impact of such an event, most people in this situation would rather transfer the risk of premature death to an insurance company because they would never want to be such a burden on other people. Since risk transfer is a fairly complex topic and the decisions we make in this area have a huge impact on our personal finances, we will discuss these issues in greater depth in the next chapter.

4. Retaining Risk

If we do not make a conscious decision to avoid or transfer a risk, then by default we retain it, accepting full responsibility for the potential loss. In some cases, retaining a risk is no big deal. In other cases, retaining a risk could completely devastate us. Retention is the most suitable approach when the potential severity of a loss is low, regardless of how frequently it is expected to occur, or if the cost of insuring the risk would be higher over time than the actual potential loss incurred.

A great example of this is total replacement coverage for a cell phone. When recently upgrading my wife's cell phone, I chuckled at what our service provider was offering. The monthly payment for their total replacement insurance plan would be enough for me to buy her a brand new phone in less than two years. Under the terms of this plan, to receive a replacement phone she would also have to pay a deductible of about half the original cost of the phone. We decided that if something did happen to her phone, it would not hurt too much to simply buy a new one, so we chose to retain the risk ourselves by not purchasing the replacement plan.

Risk retention typically is not the best strategy if the potential severity of a loss is high, even if the probability of loss is low, such as the risk of incurring hundreds of thousands of dollars worth of medical bills due to life-threatening injury or illness. When we retain a risk, we must be prepared to finance the loss ourselves.

Trying to retain high severity risks often results in less efficient use of significant resources, such as too much money in a liquid savings account that could be earning more in other investments. Another cost associated with retaining risk may include lost productivity due to unnecessary stress and worry. When we choose to retain risk but do not know for sure whether we could absorb the potential loss, we may become debilitated by fear.

Risk retention in moderation can be a prudent approach when properly combined with risk transfer, in the form of high deductibles on insurance coverage. Low deductibles can actually be very expensive because they typically require much higher premiums without providing much benefit. High deductibles can significantly reduce insurance premiums while still making the impact of large losses affordable.

When to Utilize Each Option

How can we know which of the four risk management approaches is the best for any given risk? Prudent principles dictate the following:

1. If the expected frequency and loss severity of a risk are high, we should *avoid* the risk, because retaining or insuring the risk would be far too expensive.
2. If the expected frequency is low but the potential loss severity is high, we should *transfer* the risk to a third party, such as an insurance company.
3. If the expected loss severity of a risk is low, regardless of how frequently it may occur, we should *retain* the risk.
4. When retaining or transferring a risk, we should also *reduce* the potential frequency and severity of losses as much as possible.

These rules are summarized in the chart below for easy reference:

	Low Severity	High Severity
Low Frequency	Retain	Transfer
High Frequency	Retain	Avoid

Here are some specific examples of real-life scenarios for each category:

	Low Severity	High Severity
Low Frequency	Paying out of pocket to fix chip in windshield	Income loss due to long-term illness or injury
Low Frequency	Covering repairs from minor auto accidents	Income loss due to premature death
High Frequency	Paying out of pocket for routine physicals	Loss of money to gambling or ultra-risky investing
High Frequency	Covering the cost of minor illness or injury	Bankruptcy due to excessive amounts of debt

Often it makes sense to utilize a combination of techniques to manage a particular risk. For example, to return to our driving example, we could refuse to drive at night if we have poor eyesight (avoiding risk), always wear seatbelts and obey traffic laws (reducing risk), maintain high liability limits on auto insurance (transferring risk), and choose high deductibles to decrease insurance premiums (retaining risk).

Once we are aware of the biggest threats to our financial security and have decided which of the four risk management techniques we will employ to address each risk, we can be at peace knowing that we did the best we could. We will have a plan in place so we no longer have to worry about how we would cope if disaster struck.

5

Transfer Big Risks

The Right Types of Insurance

In this chapter we will take a closer look at the most effective ways to transfer risk to insurance companies. Have you ever felt like you were over-insured? No one wants to waste money on unnecessary insurance premiums because every dollar wasted is a dollar that could have been invested or spent on something a lot more exciting than insurance.

On the other hand, not having the right types or amounts of insurance can be very detrimental to wealth building and enjoyment of life. How can we find the proper balance? The key is to cover only the potentially catastrophic risks we cannot completely avoid. The following types of insurance cover risks in that category:

1. Auto Insurance
2. Homeowners Insurance
3. Umbrella Liability Insurance
4. Medical Insurance
5. Long Term Disability Insurance
6. Long Term Care Insurance
7. Life Insurance

These types of insurance are critical because uninsured losses we may experience in these areas have the potential to financially devastate us. For example, if we carried only the minimum required auto insurance liability limits and seriously injured or killed someone in a car accident, how would we pay for the vehicle damage, medical expenses, and income loss of the other driver, which could add up to hundreds of thousands, even millions of dollars? How could we pay medical bills for unexpected cancer treatments, surgeries, and long-term hospital confinement if we had no medical insurance?

Many years ago I met a man in his fifties who had incurred hundreds of thousands of dollars in medical bills twenty years earlier because his wife had developed a serious illness at a time when they had no medical insurance. She eventually recovered physically, but he told me he does not think they will ever fully recover financially from the effects of that huge unexpected blow. He pleaded, "Make sure you always carry medical insurance for your family and tell all your clients to do the same. I severely underestimated the potential for medical bills to wipe us out financially for the rest of our lives."

If we choose not to have insurance in any of the areas listed above, we need to create a realistic plan for how we would cope if disaster struck. For example, if we choose not to acquire disability insurance, we would be foolish to say, "I do not need it because I am never going to get sick or hurt." Of course no one ever plans to get sick or hurt. It happens when we least expect it.

A realistic alternative plan might be the following: "If I cannot work because of sickness or injury, we will move in with my in-laws and use our retirement and college savings to pay for my wife to go back to school so she can earn enough to support us. We will no longer help our children pay for their college education, and we will postpone retirement for another 10-15 years beyond what we originally planned for." If we cannot think of an alternative plan that is realistic and acceptable to us and those who financially depend on us, then transferring the risk to an insurance company might be the best strategy.

In my opinion every other kind of personal insurance is optional: dental insurance, short term disability insurance, accident insurance, home warranties, extended warranties on cars and appliances, credit insurance, travel insurance, and many others. These are nice to have if someone else is paying for them, but the premiums tend to be very high for the benefits provided, and no loss in any of these areas has the potential to ruin us financially. Therefore, if we are underinsured in the essential areas but are paying for coverage in optional areas, it may be wise to terminate nonessential coverage and use the premium savings to increase critical coverage.

The Right Amounts of Insurance

How can we know how much is the right amount for each type of essential insurance? The short answer is as much as the insurance company is willing to give us, for the lowest possible cost. I want full replacement value for all of my most valuable assets. If my home burns to the ground, I want the insurance company to pay to rebuild the whole house, not just the kitchen. If they would not rebuild my house the way it was before the fire, what is the point of even having insurance? I also want to retain as much of the risk as I can afford to retain through high deductibles so my premiums will be as low as possible without sacrificing high coverage limits.

Although everyone's insurance needs are unique and should be reviewed by a competent advisor, here are some general guidelines for each type of coverage:

1. Auto Insurance

Liability limits are the biggest priority. I normally recommend the highest available liability limits, which are typically $250,000/500,000/100,000, and the highest available deductible, which is usually $1,000. If your coverage is currently significantly lower than this, you may be surprised to discover how inexpensive dramatically increasing your coverage will be, especially when you simultaneously raise your deductibles.

2. Homeowners Insurance

Be sure your home is insured for full replacement cost, but no more. You should periodically ask your agent to complete an updated replacement cost estimate to determine whether your coverage needs to be adjusted. Keep in mind that your home may need to be insured for more than it is currently worth because replacement cost is not directly related to market value, rather the estimated cost of labor and materials for rebuilding your home from scratch. I also recommend the highest available liability limits and at least a $1,000 deductible.

Most homeowners insurance policies automatically come equipped with plenty of general personal property coverage. However, watch out for exclusions and limitations on certain types of personal property. Typically insurance companies will not pay much for stolen or damaged jewelry, musical instruments, art work, or other valuable collectibles unless you add an endorsement to specifically cover these items for their full value. It might also be helpful to keep receipts, pictures, or videos of your personal belongings in a safe place offsite so you could easily prove to an insurance adjuster what you are entitled to in the case of a loss.

3. Umbrella Liability Insurance

What is an umbrella? It covers any personal liability that exceeds the limits of auto and homeowners insurance policies. It also covers other types of personal liability, such as libel or slander, but does not cover business-related activities. Coverage options range from $1,000,000 to $10,000,000. Typically I recommend at least $1,000,000 for people making a good income even if they do not yet own many assets, to help prevent the risk of their wages being garnished in the case of a major judgment against them. Of course people with substantial assets may be wise to acquire higher limits relative to their net worth.

Does that seem excessive? Wouldn't a $250,000 liability limit per person be more than enough to cover any auto accident? True, it would cover most accidents, but not every accident.

What if the person you hit is killed or sustains injuries so severe that she cannot work for the rest of her life? How much should her family be entitled to receive? That depends on her age and income.

Let's say she is 35 years old and makes $100,000 a year. Would it be unreasonable to suggest that she could have worked at least another 20 years if you had not hit her? Income of $100,000 per year for 20 years would be at least $2,000,000 total potential income lost. What about the cost of medical expenses, pain and suffering, and vehicle damage, on top of the income loss? What would you want for your family if you were the victim in this situation? Would you be greedy for wanting at least $2,000,000, or would that be reasonable compensation for your loss? I think it would be totally reasonable, and so do the courts.

4. Medical Insurance

At the time of this writing, our country is going through a major health care crisis. For many years it has been common for employers to provide medical insurance to their employees at no cost or very little cost. However, since medical insurance premiums have skyrocketed over the past several years and businesses have struggled to maintain profitability, many employers are requiring their employees to bear a much higher portion of the cost or are dropping coverage completely.

If your employer still provides medical insurance benefits at a nominal cost, I strongly recommend that you take it. If you are self-employed, or if your employer no longer provides these benefits, you need to get your own policy. Even though you will probably pay much higher premiums for this coverage than for any of the other essential types of insurance, it is critical to have.

To help mitigate the cost, you may want to consider a high-deductible major medical plan, maybe even with a $5,000 or $10,000 deductible. Remember that we are not trying to make the insurance company pay for every little prescription and doctor's visit. We just want them to handle the enormously expensive services, such as major surgeries or long-term hospital stays, so we do not lose everything if we incur a serious injury or illness. You might feel like these plans are a rip-off at first if you are used to small co-pays because you will have to pay the full cost of everything until you meet your deductible. However, you may be surprised to discover that the cost of most doctor visits are not much higher than the co-pays, and chances are you will come out ahead.

If you do go with a high-deductible plan, be sure to also sign up for a Health Savings Account (H.S.A.), which allows you to make tax-deductible contributions up to a certain limit each year

($6,150 per family in 2011). Then you can take tax-free distributions from your H.S.A. to pay for qualified medical expenses.

5. Long Term Disability Insurance

What is your most valuable asset? Is it your house? Your 401(k)? Your savings account? For most people, although they may not realize it, their biggest asset by far is their ability to earn an income. If their earned income were to stop, their whole life would fall apart.

If you make $250,000 per year and plan to work another 20 years, your ability to earn an income is worth at least $5,000,000. If your income goes up by only 3% per year, then you will have earned more than $6,700,000 total over 20 years. How does that compare to the value of your house, which many people think is their biggest asset?

Let's say your house is currently worth $500,000. That would equal only two years of your current income. If it appreciates by 3% over the next 20 years, then the value would grow to a little over $900,000, which is less than one-seventh of the total value of your earned income over that same time period.

What are you doing now to protect your ability to earn an income? Could you afford to take a two-year vacation right now? If not, how would you cope if you could not work for two years or longer because of sickness or injury? The most practical and economic solution might be a long-term disability insurance policy, unless you already receive enough passive investment income to meet all of your obligations without working.

Would you ever buy a house without insuring it? Most people would not, even though the chances of a total loss are extremely low, and the financial impact of having to pay out of pocket to rebuild it themselves would not be nearly as devastating as losing their income for several years would be. What are the odds of not being able to work for an extended period due to sickness or injury? Much higher than the probability of your home burning down, and the consequences would be far more devastating. Therefore, I recommend that you acquire the maximum amount of disability insurance for which you can qualify.

According to the Council for Disability Awareness, a healthy 35-year-old male working in an office job with some outdoor physical responsibilities has a 21% chance of becoming disabled for three months or longer during his working career. The average length of disability for men in that category is almost seven years.[8] The likelihood of incurring a disability is even higher for men who are older or not as healthy. Over 90% of disabilities are caused by illness, not accident, so people with low-risk office jobs like mine are not immune to potential income loss due to disability.[9]

Most insurance companies will replace 50-70% of lost income, depending on your annual income and profession. However, if the premiums are paid with after-tax dollars, the benefit is 100% tax-free, so a 60% benefit might feel more like an 80% replacement of take-home pay. Be sure to choose a long benefit period (to age 65 or longer), long elimination period (90 days or longer), inflation-adjusted benefit (COLA), and residual rider that will pay a portion of your benefit if you are working part-time. Also be sure that your policy covers your specific occupation for the rest of your life and that it is non-cancelable, which means the premiums can never be increased for any reason.

6. Long Term Care Insurance

While disability insurance protects income, long term care insurance protects assets. It pays for nursing home, assisted living, home health care, and other related expenses if you have severe cognitive impairment or if you cannot perform two out of the following six "Activities of Daily Living" without assistance: bathing, dressing, eating, using the toilet, transferring (to or from a bed or chair), and caring for incontinence. If your assets are getting close to the point of generating enough income for you to be able to discontinue working, this may be a more critical issue to consider than disability insurance.

The cost of long term care services has increased dramatically over the past several years at a rate much higher than the general rate of inflation. These costs are expected to continue increasing as baby boomers grow older and place greater demand on these services, and as people continue to live longer. Therefore, long term care expenses have become one of the greatest threats to retirement income security and legacy objectives. While life insurance protects your family if you die too soon, long term care insurance protects your family if you live "too long" because it helps prevent the depletion of your assets to cover long term care expenses.

According to the U.S. Department of Health and Human Services in 2012, "About 70 percent of people over age 65 will require some type of long-term care services during their lifetime. More than 40 percent will need care in a nursing home. On average, someone who is 65 today will need some type of long-term care services and supports for three years."[10] Some people require these services for much longer.

In 2011 the median annual cost nationwide for a private room in a nursing home was $77,745, which is $213 per day, so I would recommend at least that much coverage in long term care insurance for those who are eligible. In 2005 the median annual cost was only $60,225. The 2011 rate represents an average increase of 4.35% per year since 2005, so be sure your policy includes at least a 5% compound inflation rider.[11]

Why not just let Medicare or Medicaid pay for it? Unfortunately, Medicare does not cover most long term care expenses. To qualify for Medicaid in most states, you can only own about $3,000 in assets other than your personal residence and personal belongings, and can only be receiving about $2,000 per month in income.[12] Both programs are desperately struggling to stay afloat, so I expect benefits to be cut even further in the future.

Long term care insurance provides just as many emotional benefits as financial. It helps to preserve a strong marriage because it allows the healthy spouse to maintain her own well-being by serving as care manager rather than care giver. Some policies provide concierge-type services that research the best local providers and arrange every aspect of care needed so the insured does not have to hassle with it. Couples who carry adequate long term care insurance are more likely to continue living a better quality of life throughout retirement because they will not feel guilty about receiving quality care they may need. They do not have to worry as much about whether the cost of their care will deplete assets they intended to leave to a spouse or other loved ones.

7. Life Insurance

Are you worth more dead than alive? How much is the right amount of life insurance? I have found that although most people realize the importance of life insurance, they do not give much thought to how much is the right amount for their situation.

Most people also assume that they could purchase as much life insurance as they want. You may be surprised to learn that insurance companies actually will not allow you to be worth more dead than alive. No asset can be insured for more than its current economic value, whether it is a car, a house, or a human life.

The amount of life insurance for which you can qualify is based on your current age, annual income, assets, and debts. This is called your "human life value," and it represents the economic loss which those who are financially dependent upon you would suffer if you were to pass away, such as family members, business partners, or creditors. Similar calculations based on age and income are also used by the courts to determine appropriate wrongful death awards, and were used by the administrators of the September 11th Victim Compensation Fund to determine how much should be paid to the family members of those who had been killed in the terrorist attacks of September 11, 2001.

Of course the economic loss is only a tiny sliver of the total loss suffered when a human life is lost. The value of a human spirit could never be fully replaced. Each person's talents, love, experience, wisdom, example, creativity, future capacity to give, and service to society are irreplaceable. That is why each of us will always be worth more alive than dead, no matter how much life insurance we carry. The only thing insurance can do is help to compensate for the economic loss. Thus, fully insuring our human life value is the least we can do for those who are dependent upon us.

The following are typical human life value calculations (insurance company underwriting guidelines for income replacement):

Age	Maximum Life Insurance
20-29	30 x income
30-39	20 x income
40-49	15 x income
50-59	10 x income
60+	5 x income

In other words, if you are 35 years old and make $100,000 per year, the total maximum amount of life insurance for which you could qualify with any combination of insurance companies is $2,000,000. If you are 45 years old and make $250,000 per year, your total available coverage is $3,750,000. If you are 55 years old and make $500,000 per year, the max you can get is $5,000,000, and so on. Unless you own substantial assets, I recommend acquiring a life insurance death benefit equal to your full human life value in order to provide adequate income replacement for your family. It is not merely a debt payoff tool.

Non-working spouses also make a significant economic contribution to the family even if they do not earn an income. Have you ever thought about how much it would cost to hire other people to do everything your spouse does for your family if he or she were to pass away? In addition, maybe you would want to work fewer hours so you could take over some of those roles yourself and spend more time with your kids. Therefore, it is also important to acquire life insurance on a non-working spouse, especially if you have children living at home. The maximum amount for which a non-working spouse can qualify is usually around half the amount the working spouse carries.

Human life value can also be determined by a person's net worth, which is the difference between total assets and total liabilities. For estate planning purposes, insurance companies are usually willing to offer a death benefit equal to the net worth of an individual if it would result in a higher death benefit than the income calculations listed above.

After you have determined the appropriate amount of life insurance, you must also determine which type is best for you, both in the short run and in the long run. This decision will have a huge impact on your financial well-being throughout your life.

Term insurance (temporary insurance) has the lowest initial premium but the highest long-term cost because premiums increase over time and your beneficiaries are highly unlikely to ever collect any payout from it. Premium payment terms are very inflexible and you never receive any of your premiums back.

Whole life insurance (permanent insurance) has the highest initial premium but the lowest long-term cost because premiums never increase, and your beneficiaries are guaranteed to receive a much higher payout than what you put into it, as long as the policy stays in force. Furthermore, whole life insurance provides living benefits to you because it builds liquid cash that you can access at any time for any purpose. In the long run, the cash available for you to spend while you are alive is highly likely to be worth much more than what you put into it. Since it builds accessible cash, whole life premium payments count towards your 20% savings goal. Thus, you can accomplish both protection and asset building objectives at once.

The optimum solution would be to own some of each—a prudent amount of whole life insurance depending on how much you are currently allocating to savings, and the rest in term insurance up to your full human life value. Remember that the amount is initially more important than the type. If current cash flow only enables you to acquire term insurance for your full human life value, then just do that for now. Resist the temptation to acquire a smaller death benefit than your family really needs just so you can have some whole life insurance. You can gradually convert portions of your term insurance to whole life later as you increase your savings and eliminate debt.

Some advisors always recommend term insurance and never recommend whole life, emphasizing the initial difference in premiums. They argue that term insurance is a better deal because the premiums are lower. On the surface this may appear to be true, but obviously it does not tell the whole story.

Which do you think would be better for your situation? Why not own some of each like I do for myself and my family, since they each do a great job performing their intended function? (See charts on the next two pages.)

Term Insurance (Temporary)

Advantages	Disadvantages
1. Premiums are initially much lower than for whole life insurance. 2. Great for acquiring a large amount of coverage for a temporary period when money is tight, especially for young families. 3. Adequately meets temporary needs such as funding a buy-sell agreement or when life insurance is required for a loan approval.	1. It is very likely to expire before you actually use it. 2. It ends up costing a lot more than whole life insurance would have cost if held until the age of normal life expectancy. 3. You do not get any of your money back if you cancel the policy before you die. 4. Premium payment terms have no flexibility. The death benefit expires after 30 days of nonpayment. 5. If you are allowed to keep the policy after the initial lock-in period, the premiums dramatically increase every year afterward, but the death benefit does not increase.

Whole Life Insurance (Permanent)

Advantages	Disadvantages
1. Death benefit is guaranteed for your entire lifetime, as long as premiums are paid.	1. The premium is much higher than for term insurance in the early years.
2. Death benefit increases over time with the payment of dividends, but the premium never increases.	2. The cash value liquidity is low in the first few years. It takes time to build equity.
3. Eventually you may be able to stop paying premiums and maintain the death benefit for the rest of your life.[13]	
4. In the long run, you get all of your premium payments back plus a healthy rate of return.	
5. Builds cash value that may be withdrawn tax-free for any purpose, at any age, during your lifetime.[14]	
6. Cash value has built-in guarantees that are not subject to market volatility.	
7. Cash value may be protected from lawsuit, depending on which state you live in.	
8. Waiver of premium feature allows your cash value to continue growing even if you cannot work due to sickness or injury for six months or more.[15]	

Gambling vs. Insurance

Some people think that buying insurance is like gambling. They say that if we end up using it, we win and the insurance company loses. If we never end up using it, we lose and the insurance company wins.

However, buying insurance is actually very different from gambling. When we enter into a gambling engagement, such as buying a lottery ticket or putting money in a slot machine, we create risk of loss that did not previously exist. In other words, there was no risk of losing money to gambling until we bought the lottery ticket or put the money in the slot machine.

Conversely, the risk of financial loss from other causes already exists whether we purchase insurance or not. For example, my home faces the same risk of being burned down by a fire whether I buy homeowners insurance or not. If I do not have homeowners insurance, I am faced with the possibility of having to pay completely out of my pocket to rebuild my home in the event of a fire.

Even if we never end up using our insurance, we still benefit from it because it enables us to live a full, fun, free life that is unencumbered by constant fear of loss. If insurance did not exist, we may not feel comfortable buying or doing many of the things we now consider to be no big deal. When we are properly insured, we feel free to buy expensive homes, drive our own cars down the freeway, fly to Hawaii, cruise through the mountains on ATVs, ski down black diamond runs, and maybe even hike through the rainforests of South America.

Have you ever driven across the majestic San Francisco-Oakland Bay Bridge that spans the San Francisco Bay in California? It is very impressive. According to the California Department of Transportation, it is 4.5 miles long (one of the longest spans in the world), 5 lanes wide, and stands about 200 feet above the water level of the bay. On average, 280,000 vehicles use the Bay Bridge per day. The speed limit for most of the bridge is 50 MPH, so thankfully it is equipped with hefty guard-rails on each side.[16]

For those of you who have driven across the Bay Bridge, have you ever hit one of the guardrails? I am sure that a very small percentage of the 280,000 vehicles that cross the bridge every day have ever hit the guardrails. However, if the guardrails were removed, how fast do you think people would drive across the bridge, even though they have never needed to use the guardrails in the past? 20 MPH? 10 MPH? Some of you may quip that you have never been able to drive more than 10 MPH over the bridge anyway because you are always crossing at rush hour, but you get my point.

Even if no one ever hits them, the presence of the guardrails still improves the lives of everyone who crosses the bridge because they can enjoy the drive without having to worry about falling into the water, and they can drive much faster than they would dare to drive otherwise. Would any of these passengers argue that building the guardrails was a waste of money?

Much like guardrails, insurance benefits our lives by increasing our efficiency and reducing our fear, even if we never end up using it. We must carry adequate insurance coverage in all of the essential areas if we are serious about maintaining financial security throughout our entire lives.

6

Save Some for Later

Are You an Ant or a Grasshopper?

Remember Aesop's Fable "The Ant and the Grasshopper?" In this classic tale, a grasshopper was singing and playing away the summer days when he observed an ant working hard to store food for the winter. The grasshopper ridiculed the ant for working so hard and tried to convince him to relax. The ant declined, warning the grasshopper that he should also be preparing for the winter. The grasshopper laughed and went on his merry way, confident that there was nothing to worry about. However, when winter came, the grasshopper realized that the ant was right because he had no food and was starving to death. Are you an ant or a grasshopper?

Way too many of us live paycheck to paycheck, completely vulnerable to every little unexpected event, because we are not saving enough of our paycheck for later. Family members get sick or lose their jobs. Food and gas prices go up. Income taxes, property taxes, and sales taxes go up. Cars and appliances break down. Carpets, furniture, and roofs need to be replaced. Clothes go out of style. Computers become outdated and new smart phones come out that we *have* to buy right when they first become available. Children get married earlier than we expected or take six years to finish a four-year college degree.

Sound familiar? This is real life. We may label these as "unexpected emergencies," but how unexpected are they really? They should not come as too big of a surprise, because most of them are inevitable. We do not have to wonder "if" they will occur, rather "when" will they occur.

Virtually everything we buy is designed to break down, run out, or go out of style. Other people do not always fulfill their promises. The cost of everything is always going up. Yet we typically live our day-to-day lives in denial of these obvious facts because we want to spend more money on improving our lifestyle now and deal with our future needs later. Some people even treat Christmas shopping as an unexpected emergency, racking up thousands of dollars in high-interest credit card debt to buy presents, as if it were a surprise every year that Christmas came on December 25th again.

Control Your Own Destiny

The lack of adequate savings is the biggest reason most people are never able to get ahead financially. In order to prepare for the inevitable "unexpected" and eventually be able to retire, we must regularly save a significant portion of our current income.

How can we know how much is the right amount? Consider the following popular methods that do not work. Have you tried any of these? Have they granted you financial independence?

1. Save whatever is left over at the end of the month, after all expenses have been met.
2. Save only the minimum amount necessary in 401(k) plan at work to qualify for the employer match.
3. Save only the maximum annual amount the IRS will allow you to contribute to a 401(k) or IRA.
4. Produce a mathematical equation that dictates how much you should save, based on arbitrary assumptions made concerning the following variables:
    a. Desired retirement date
    b. Desired retirement income
    c. Life expectancy
    d. Inflation rate
    e. Future tax rates
    f. Future cost of medical care
    g. Rate of return before and during retirement

The first example never works because we never have enough money to buy all the things we want, as we discussed earlier. Hence, we seldom have much money left at the end of the month to save, if any at all.

The second and third examples are not likely to result in a comfortable retirement because 401(k)s were not designed to be anyone's sole retirement savings plan, rather a supplement to pensions and other more significant retirement income platforms. The IRS maximum contribution limits alone are not adequate to produce most people's full retirement income objectives.

The fourth example often misses the mark because no one can really know what the actual figures will be for any of the variables listed above, let alone for all of them. Only one assumption has to be off by a little to produce drastically different results.

Most people underestimate the amount of income required to maintain the lifestyle they desire in retirement, how much future costs will continue to increase, and how long they will live. They also tend to overestimate the rate of return they will earn on their investments so that retirement income calculators will show them great results in the end without having to save much today. Then they are very disappointed when they discover that this strategy did not yield a great retirement because they did not earn the rate of return they were expecting.

We must not allow our current spending wants, our employer, the government, or an unreliable mathematical equation dictate how much we save. If we do not end up having enough to do what we want later in life, we will have no one to blame but ourselves. We must control our own destiny by saving much more than these failure-prone methods dictate.

How Much Should We Save?

The best way to calculate the proper amount to save is as a flat percentage of current income. I believe we all must consistently save at least 20% of our gross income if we ever want to get ahead financially and retire comfortably someday.

Everyone I have ever met who is financially independent, meaning that they have enough money to live a comfortable lifestyle without having to work, has consistently saved a significant portion of their income, many of them more than 20%. No other reliable way to accomplish this exists, except perhaps by means of an employer or government pension that guarantees payment of a significant portion of pre-retirement income for life. Still, most people I have met who are successfully living on pension income also regularly saved a large percentage of their income throughout their careers. Keep in mind that many pensions are facing severe financial difficulty, so even if we are entitled to a pension, we would be wise to save a substantial amount of our income in case it does not pay out as expected.

Consider a famous example in the Bible from thousands of years ago which illustrates the wisdom of saving at least 20% of our income. Joseph, the son of Israel who was sold by his brothers as a slave and then taken to Egypt, was the only man able to interpret Pharaoh's troubling dreams. Joseph perceived that the dreams were actually warnings from God that there would be seven years of plenty followed by seven years of famine.

Joseph counseled Pharaoh to save a fifth part (20%) of all the food that was grown during the seven years of plenty so they would be prepared to survive the seven years of famine. Pharaoh followed Joseph's advice, and everything occurred as he predicted. The Egyptians successfully survived the seven years of famine (see Genesis 41).

What can we learn from this example? Do we experience modern-day famines for which we need to prepare? Absolutely! One such famine could be called a "market decline." Another could be called a "soft job market." Haven't the lingering effects of the Great Recession of 2008-2009 felt much like a modern-day famine? How different would things have turned out if we had all been saving 20% of our income instead of spending more than we made for several years leading up to the market crash of 2008?

The problem was not the fact that the market declined. Market declines have occurred often enough throughout history for us to know that they are to be expected. Although their timing and magnitude is unpredictable, they are simply a normal part of the economic cycle. The market crash of 2008 just happened to be a particularly dramatic decline because so many people, businesses, and governments were overleveraged and underprepared for the downturn. If everyone had been living on less than they made and saving 20% of their income, the decline would not have been nearly as severe.

The government has created all sorts of new legislation to try to prevent a similar tragedy from occurring again, but as long as greed and dishonesty exist, it will happen again. Hopefully next time it happens some of us will be better prepared for it. If we are prepared, we may actually experience it as a great investment opportunity rather than as a personal tragedy.

The famine in Egypt so long ago turned out to be an opportunity for Pharaoh to increase his wealth because he was so well prepared. Not only did he have enough to provide for himself and his people, but he also had sufficient surplus to sell corn to many starving people who came to him from surrounding regions because they were not prepared for the famine.

We have seen this same phenomenon during the Great Recession among those who were prepared. People who still had a lot of money after the crash because they were frugal in their expenditures and conservative with their investments while most other people were spending up a storm and taking tons of risk are now making a killing buying up real estate and other investments at very low prices. There is more money to be made during the bad times than during the good times for those who are prepared to capture the opportunity.

When things are going well, we have the tendency to believe they will always continue to go well. That is why we buy the biggest houses and the most expensive cars the banks will let us qualify for based on our current income. The minute our income goes up, we think we are entitled to even bigger and better things.

Would we buy such a big house if we knew that starting seven years from now we would be unemployed for seven years? How much of our current income would we be saving in preparation for such a famine? Would we be more motivated to curtail our spending habits?

Saving at least 20% of our income no matter what, and then living joyfully on the rest, gives us the shock absorbers we need when the good times stop rolling, and gives us hope for a comfortable retirement someday. If we are doing exceptionally well, we may choose to save much more than 20%. The Bible says, "And Joseph gathered corn as the sand of the sea, very much, until he left numbering; for it was without number" (Genesis 41:49). The more we save, the better off we will be in the future.

Slow and Steady Wins the Race

Often when I meet with people who are learning these principles for the first time, they are anxious to get started and want to do everything perfectly right away. I am glad for their enthusiasm, but this approach may not be sustainable. I would not normally recommend that people immediately start saving 20% of their income if they are only accustomed to saving 5%. That would be like trying to run a full marathon if they had never run more than six miles at a time. Marathon trainers recommend starting with a much shorter distance than the full 26.2 miles, then adding no more than 10% to the training distance each week. Otherwise, trainees could injure themselves and lose months of progress.

Likewise, too big of a sudden increase in savings could cause "financial injuries" such as increased credit card debt, marriage tension, or spending binges. We may even become so frustrated that we stop saving completely. Of course any level of savings requires some sacrifice, but starting with a realistic amount that does not hurt too much is more healthy and sustainable. Then we can gradually increase it over time.

Those who are not saving anything at all right now might even want to try starting with only 1-2% of income. Most people are surprised how little they feel the difference when they increase their savings by modest amounts. Then gradually building from there is easier. Just remember that whatever amount we decide to save now, in the future we are likely to wish we had saved more.

A great time to increase the percentage of income that we save is when we get a raise, bonus, second job, or pay off a debt, before we get used to spending the higher net income. We should not feel obligated to save all of our increase, though. We should celebrate our successes by spending some of those nice income boosts along the way on fun things we have been craving. This practice will help motivate us to continue moving forward.

Occasionally I meet with people whose income just increased dramatically, even by as much as four or five times their former income, or who just paid off some very large debts. That is a perfect time to immediately start saving a much higher percentage of income before growing accustomed to spending at higher levels.

What if we are spending more than we make each month and not saving anything? The first step is to stop spending so much. If we continue down that road, eventually we will end up bankrupt.

Remember the disastrous oil spill in the Gulf of Mexico in 2010? Before any meaningful clean-up efforts could be started, the gushing of oil into the Gulf had to be terminated by completely capping the well. Likewise, any efforts to clean up our debt would be futile if we do not first stop disastrous leaks in our spending plan by learning to spend less than we make.

Short, frantic bursts of occasional effort to save a lot of money or pay off debts do not result in a lifetime of financial security. Getting out of debt and becoming financially secure are a lot like losing weight and becoming physically fit. If I starve myself for a few weeks, I may lose some weight, but I would gain it all back again if I do not permanently practice healthier eating habits. I may build some muscle by working out three hours one day a week, but I would produce much better results by working out just thirty minutes each day for six days a week.

Financial security is the result of a lifetime of healthy financial attitudes and behavior. It is a slow, gradual process, not a one-time event. Minor cash flow allocation adjustments make a big difference in results over time, just as an airplane pilot correcting her course by only a few degrees can make a difference of many miles over the course of an entire flight. Anyone who consistently saves 20% of income and does not incur any new debts will eventually have plenty of assets and no debt. It is inevitable.

Work as a Team

Whatever percentage you decide to allocate to savings or any other category, be sure to communicate openly with your spouse about it if you are married. You must both be in total agreement regarding where the money should go. Otherwise, your financial goals will not be sustainable and they will cause great conflict in your marriage. If you are too dictatorial, your spouse is likely to willfully undermine your efforts. If you are too secretive, he or she may unknowingly nullify your efforts.

Remember that several studies show financial discord as a leading cause for divorce. If you do not respect your spouse enough to include him or her in the planning, he or she may eventually walk away with half of the assets you were trying to build anyway. Those who communicate openly, frequently, and respectfully with their spouse tend to avoid major financial problems in their marriage.

Meeting with a competent financial planner can help foster open communication among spouses. Often couples tell me that our meetings were very therapeutic because they learned a lot about their spouse's attitude towards money and I helped them find a happy middle ground in making financial decisions. Sometimes they even apologize for turning me into a marriage counselor. Of course no apology is necessary because helping in such a meaningful way is very rewarding.

This tends to be a common response among couples because most have never discussed their deep financial values, goals, and concerns so openly with each other. Having meaningful, respectful conversations about such emotional financial issues can be very healing and bonding for couples.

Pay Off Debts Before Saving?

Often people ask me whether they should pay off all debts before saving for the future or save first in hopes of earning a higher return on investments than they are paying in interest on debts. This is an age-old debate, and I have heard convincing arguments on both sides.

Some advisors recommend that we liquidate all of our savings and investments except a very small amount, even as low as $1,000, to immediately pay down as much debt as possible. Then they recommend that we use every discretionary penny from each paycheck to eliminate the remaining debts as quickly as possible. After we are completely debt-free, then we can start saving and investing for the future.

I admire people who are disciplined enough to follow this extremely aggressive strategy, but it is risky because it does not leave an adequate safety cushion. A $1,000 savings account would not be enough to cover unemployment, major unexpected expenses, or serious extended illness. What would happen to my house if I could not make my mortgage payment for six months due to unemployment? Would the bank cut me any slack because I had been paying them extra for the past year in hopes of paying my mortgage off sooner? Not likely. We should always maintain at least three to six months of living expenses in liquid savings, even if we have debt.

On the other extreme, some people recommend borrowing as much as the banks will allow and investing it all because they declare we can make more on our investments than the banks will charge in interest. Is this true? Can we really make more than what the bank is charging us? Yes, sometimes we can, but how consistently?

This philosophy is part of what caused the real estate, banking, and stock market meltdown of 2008. Before the crash, banks were willing to lend up to 20% more than the appraised value of homes. People were pulling out all of this "equity" to buy more houses on credit, invest in the stock market, or just spend it, because they thought the value of real estate would always continue to increase as it had for many years. It is obvious to everyone now that this was not sustainable, but it was not obvious at the time. Millions of people lost a lot of money as a result of this practice, and some people lost everything.

The practice of excessive borrowing to invest is part of what caused the Stock Market Crash of 1929 that preceded the Great Depression, too. A myriad of ordinary people who did not fully understand the risks involved were buying stocks on margin, which means they were borrowing money to buy stocks they could not afford to buy on their own. Partially as a result of so many people buying stocks on margin, the already inflated value of the stock market was artificially pumped even higher during the late 1920s.

When the market started to fall, the margins were called, which means these investors were required to immediately pay the loans back in full. Since most people could not afford to re-pay these loans, they were forced to sell their stocks to meet the margin calls, which drove the already declining stock prices into a rapid downward spiral. History has taught us that maxing out our debt to invest can be very dangerous for individuals and for society as a whole.

I do not advocate either of these two extremes, but rather prefer a balanced approach. First of all, we must be careful not to become so obsessed with paying off debts or building assets that we neglect the other critical areas of taxes, tithing, protection, and maintaining adequate liquid savings. After we have acquired adequate insurance and enough liquid savings to cover three to six months of living expenses, our first priority should be to pay off high-interest short-term consumer debt such as credit cards or car loans, maybe even before investing at all. We can never get ahead financially if we consistently earn 6% on our investments while paying 18% interest on credit card debts.

After paying off all high-interest debt, we would be prudent to build assets while gradually paying off any remaining low-interest, potentially tax-deductible debt such as mortgages and student loans. Why not pay off all debts first? I have seen too many people fall into the trap of thinking that reducing debt is the same as building assets. In reality it is just making up for past overspending, unless the debt was incurred to buy assets, such as rental real estate. They think they are making financial progress by paying more than the minimum due each month. However, once they are debt-free they discover that they can afford an even bigger house, nicer car, and more toys, all of which are much more exciting than investing for the future, so they incur more debt and the cycle starts all over again.

After a few of these cycles, they arrive at retirement age wondering what happened to all those years of sacrifice to aggressively pay off their debts. Now they have nothing to show for it but memories of old cars, boats, and houses that are long gone because they were never really building assets. They were just playing a never-ending game of catch-up from former overspending.

Another reason to build assets while paying down debt is that putting everything towards debt elimination can be discouraging, especially if it is going to take a very long time to completely extinguish all debt. Conversely, seeing our assets increase while our debts are decreasing is motivating.

Building liquid assets also increases our overall safety and liquidity so we can continue to meet our obligations if our income decreases dramatically for an extended period, as in the example of unemployment we discussed earlier. If we do not have assets to tap into when times get tough, paying extra principal on a mortgage or student loan can actually be a very risky place to put money because those extra payments can never be taken back out. The extra payments do not benefit us until the loan is paid off completely. We could be making extra principal payments for ten years and then lose our job, yet the amount due the very next month would be the same as if we had never paid any extra principal. Therefore, it might be wise to continue building assets while paying down low-interest debt over time for psychological and safety reasons, even if it does not always make sense mathematically.

Amount Saved Trumps Rate of Return

According to the U.S. Department of Commerce, at the time of this writing the average monthly Personal Saving Rate in our country is about 5%.[17] No wonder the average American citizen feels like they can never get ahead financially.

What would a 5% savings rate do for a 35-year-old planning to work until age 65? Let's say she earns $100,000 per year and receives a 3% raise every year. If she can earn an 8% average annual return on her investments, in 30 years she would have accumulated about $824,000. Is that enough to retire?

Most advisors would agree that with inflation, rising health care costs, potentially rising tax rates, and increasing life expectancy, $824,000 would not even come close to meeting what someone making $100,000 today would probably expect for retirement income in 30 years. What are the alternatives?

Some advisors might suggest that she should take more risk in order to earn a higher potential return. The key word here is "potential." Sure, a 10% return would be great if she could count on it, but history has taught us that high-risk investments often end up yielding the lowest actual returns. What if her account value is chopped in half the year before she planned to retire because she was taking too much risk? This happened to many people in 2008.

Even if she could consistently earn a significantly higher return, would that really solve the problem? If she did earn a 10% average annual return over those 30 years then she would have accumulated about $1,180,000—only $356,000 more than at 8%, but with much more volatility.

As an alternative, what if she targeted a more conservative 6% return and saved 20% of her income instead of 5%? Then in 30 years she would have accumulated about $2,343,000, which is $1,519,000 more than in the first example. Can you believe the difference in results? She would also be much more likely to attain her goal and would be more at peace about how her investments are performing all along the way, since she would be taking a lot less risk.

This demonstrates that our potential to build wealth is more dependent on how much we save than on the rate of return we achieve. This is good news, because the amount we save is a lot easier to control.

Where Should We Put Our Money?

Although the amount we save is likely to have a bigger impact on our well-being than how we invest our money, we still need to invest it wisely. Choosing among the myriad of savings and investment options available can be overwhelming. How can we know where is the best place to put our money?

Countless financial institutions are constantly clamoring for us to park a piece of our pie with them. Why? That is how they make money. Unless we bury our money in the backyard, someone is going to make money off of our money no matter where we park it, even if it merely sits in a bank account. This is not a problem as long as we receive the benefits we expect in return. In order to be sure that the financial institutions meet our objectives and not just their own, we must be clear about what we are trying to accomplish with each dollar we deposit.

My motto for savings and investment advice is "safety before speed." Would you buy a car that can go from zero to sixty miles per hour in less than three seconds if it were not also equipped with excellent brakes, seat belts, and air bags? The potential rate of acceleration is much less important than the ability to avoid or minimize the impact of a crash. Without the safety elements, you may never reach your destination, no matter how fast you can go.

Money works the same way. Many people lose the opportunity to be financially secure for the rest of their lives in an effort to shortcut the process by taking too much risk with their investments. Have you ever heard the adage, "High risk equals high reward?" Is that really true?

A friend of mine told me about someone he knows who was a very aggressive real estate investor. During the boom he had acquired tens of millions of dollars worth of assets, but he got so caught up in the game that he could not slow down. In my friend's words, "He couldn't see that he was headed straight for a brick wall, and kept his pedal to the metal right up until he slammed into it. Every penny of his was invested in these high-risk assets, so when the real estate market crashed, he lost everything."

Sure, we may never be able to obtain super-high returns without taking any risk, but we must remember that investments with the highest potential returns often end up yielding the lowest actual returns. Warren Buffet, one of the most successful investors of all time, counseled, "Rule No. 1: Never lose money. Rule No. 2: Never forget Rule No. 1."

The first step to wealth building is to create a solid foundation of safe money that we can access anytime without penalties, equivalent to at least three to six months of current living expenses. For those who are self-employed or whose income is volatile, six months or more is even better.

FDIC-insured money market or regular savings accounts are ideal for this purpose. The rate of return does not matter as much as the surety that it will always be there when we need it. We should not make it too easily accessible, though, or we may be tempted to spend it on frivolous items. My wife and I like to keep our money market account at a different bank from where we hold our primary checking accounts so we do not see the balance very often. This keeps it out of mind and makes it feel a little less accessible.

We also would be wise to maintain some food and water storage, hard cash, and a 72-hour kit in case a natural disaster or other regional crisis might interrupt the general availability of basic life-sustaining commodities. Millions of dollars in the bank may not do us any good during such an event. Ideally we should have stocked up at least three months' worth of what we would normally eat.

The next step is to build assets that have a higher potential rate of return and may also give us other benefits such as creditor protection and tax savings. With this step we are not necessarily looking for a super high rate of return, but more than what we would gain in a savings account. Some examples might include 401(k)s, IRAs, non-qualified mutual funds, bonds, annuities, or whole life insurance.

After we have established a solid foundation of less risky assets, then we can invest in more speculative opportunities that have the potential to produce very high returns. Some people never want to invest speculatively because they hate the thought of losing money. That's fine—we can build significant wealth without ever investing speculatively. However, if we have a large foundation of stable assets, we might be able to afford to take more risk with a small portion of our investments in hopes of high rewards.

Why doesn't everyone take this approach? The problem is that it is not very exciting and it takes patience. I have seen many people lose the majority of their assets when times got tough because they were trying to make all of their money grow as quickly as possible, with very little regard for safety of principle.

The saddest thing about this is that many of these investors did not understand the true risk associated with these "high-performing" assets. For example, when real estate was booming, many people were investing significant amounts of money in first and second trust deeds, where the developer would typically "guarantee" a 12-16% annual return. People thought it was safe because their investment was secured by the value of the land the developer was building the project on.

Then the unthinkable happened. When the real estate market crashed, many of these developers went bankrupt, and everyone stood in line to get a piece of what was left over. Most people I know who invested in these types of deals lost almost everything they put in because they stood in line behind too many other investors, and the true value of the land securing the note dropped significantly overnight.

I have also seen people invest in a stock right after they saw it triple in value overnight, only to watch it become practically worthless within a matter of months. Others have invested in mutual funds that boasted a 70% return the year before, but then lost 80% the year after they invested in them.

It might be exciting to watch our investments rise dramatically for a time, but I have never met anyone who enjoys the excitement of watching them crash and burn. Consider the wisdom of the famous economist Paul Samuelson, the first American to win the Nobel Memorial Prize in Economic Sciences: "Investing should be more like watching paint dry or watching grass grow. If you want excitement, take $800 and go to Las Vegas."

Managing Investment Risk

How can we successfully manage investment risk? The same principles apply here that we explored in Chapter Four about risk management:

1. Avoiding Investment Risk

We should completely avoid high severity risks that are likely to occur, such as the risk of losing all of our money through gambling or investing in penny stocks. If you feel compelled to gamble for entertainment purposes, just be sure to do so only with however much you would be willing to flush down the toilet. Don't make it your retirement savings strategy. I am opposed to gambling even for entertainment, though, because it can be very addictive and destructive, and it goes completely against the principles we discussed in Chapter Two about the importance of being wise stewards over our resources.

2. Reducing Investment Risk

We can reduce investment risk through diversification, which means that we do not put all of our eggs in one basket. Many people who think they are well-diversified really are not. For example, I have met several people who think they are very well-diversified because all of their investments are in U.S. large-cap growth stock mutual funds with a variety of fund families. Typically they are shocked when I point out that most of these funds are actually investing in the same 100 or so stocks, and that many of these stocks are very similar to each other in nature. Sure, they are more diversified than if they were investing all in one stock, but true diversification would include a much larger variety of characteristics, such as geographic areas, sizes of companies, growth stages of companies, types of products or services provided (i.e. financial services, health care, technology, consumer goods), and types of investments (i.e. stocks, bonds, cash, real estate, commodities, precious metals, options, absolute return funds), to name a few.

3. Transferring Investment Risk

For the amount of money we cannot afford to lose, we may want to transfer investment risk to large, financially stable institutions, such as profitable banks or insurance companies. How much can we not afford to lose? This would include our emergency fund of three to six months of living expenses, as well as whatever investments we plan to rely on during retirement to cover at least our basic expenses, especially if we are getting close to retirement age.

We can transfer investment risk to a bank through CDs or money market accounts, or to an insurance company through annuities or whole life insurance. CDs pay a guaranteed fixed interest rate for a specified period of time, regardless of the bank's investment performance. Money market accounts pay a variable interest rate, adjustable by the bank from time to time, but with no risk of losing principal when FDIC-insured.

Fixed annuities pay a guaranteed fixed interest rate for a specified period of time, much like a CD, regardless of the insurance company's investment performance. Variable annuities allow participation in market growth opportunities while minimizing downside risk by guaranteeing a certain amount of retirement income for life, regardless of market performance.

Whole life insurance provides guaranteed cash value and a guaranteed death benefit, regardless of the insurance company's investment performance. It can grow by more than the guaranteed amount if the insurance company does well, but it is not subject to market risk. A significant portion of the cash value may be withdrawn tax-free at any time for retirement income or other purposes, and in some states may be protected from creditors.[18]

4. Retaining Investment Risk

For the amount of money we are willing to risk losing, we may choose to retain risk by investing on our own to see if we can produce higher returns than financial institutions can guarantee for us. Of course we would still be prudent to reduce risk of losing these assets through adequate due diligence and diversification. It is also wise to invest primarily in that which we understand or over which we have some control. For example, although starting a small business is normally considered a very risky investment, it may not be as risky for someone with 20 years of successful experience working for a large corporation before starting her own business in the same field.

Maintaining Financial Balance

Do the myriad of options still sound overwhelming? This book is not meant to give a comprehensive list of every possible investment and when each would be appropriate. We are merely discussing general principles to indicate the surest path to financial security, regardless of market performance and unexpected personal crises that may occur along the way. Meeting with a qualified financial advisor is critical to determining which investment options would be best for your current situation.

We must maintain financial balance in order to maintain financial security. Each savings and investment option carries advantages and disadvantages, so we maintain balance by dividing our regular savings contributions among various opportunities with complementary characteristics. For example, we may direct a portion of our savings to a money market account because we want the safety and accessibility it provides. However, if all of our money is in money market accounts, it will never grow by much, any interest we earn will be 100% taxable, and all of it may be exposed to creditors in the case of a lawsuit.

In order to mitigate the disadvantages of money market accounts, we may want to direct a portion of our monthly savings to a 401(k) plan. By doing so we would receive a current tax deduction, tax deferred growth, greater potential returns, creditor protection, and perhaps an employer matching contribution. However, these benefits also come at a price. The greater potential returns in 401(k) plans are subject to market risk, the money we put in is not accessible without severe penalty until retirement (with a few strict exceptions), any money we pull out at retirement is 100% taxable as ordinary income, we have to start taking money out at age 70-1/2 even if we do not need it, it is 100% taxable to our heirs upon our death, and if we cannot work due to sickness or injury, we are prohibited by law to continue contributing to it.

To make up for the disadvantages of money market accounts and 401(k) plans, we might choose to increase our financial balance by also directing a portion of our savings to a whole life insurance policy. This may give us much higher long-term rates of return than a money market account without being subject to market risk, flexibility to withdraw money at any time for any purpose, creditor protection (depending on the state), a guaranteed tax-free death benefit to our heirs that never expires, and continued contributions guaranteed by the insurance company if we cannot work for six months or longer due to illness or injury.[19]

See what I mean about balance? Which option is the best? In reality none is inherently better than the other. They just perform different functions. They are often pitted against one another by some advisors as if they are in competition with each other, but it does not have to be that way. All three of these options, as well as several other options not mentioned here, can work very powerfully in harmony with one another because each provides distinct benefits that complement one another.

Realistic Expectations

Some financial talking heads preach that we should invest all of our money in growth stocks because that is what has produced the highest rate of return over the "long haul." They claim that we can count on receiving a 12% or more average annual rate of return because that has been the average return in growth stocks over the past 70 years. Is this true?

Professor Campbell R. Harvey of Duke University, who is also a research associate of the National Bureau of Economic Research, determined that if $1 had been invested in a U.S. small stock index in December 1925, with all proceeds reinvested tax-free into the same index, the account would have been worth

$3,425 in June of 1995. If that same $1 had been invested in a U.S. large stock index (S&P 500), it would be worth $974 at the end of the period. The final value would be $44 if invested in long-term corporate bonds, and only $13 if invested in U.S. Treasury Bills. In this example, the average annual rate of return over that nearly 70-year period would have been 12.4% for small stocks, 10.4% for large stocks, 5.6% for bonds, and 3.7% for T-Bills.[20]

With these statistics in mind, no wonder many advisors recommend that the majority of our money be invested in stocks. However, do we really have claim on a 70-year average rate of return? Who is able to leave their money in stocks for 70 years without touching it, paying taxes, or paying any investment management fees? That may be a mathematically correct long-term rate of return, but what is the real rate of return we may personally expect?

DALBAR Research conducted a fascinating study entitled "Quantitative Analysis of Investor Behavior," which measures the impact of investor behavior on actual returns realized by the average stock mutual fund investor. DALBAR discovered that the performance of individual investors tends to significantly lag actual index performance due to taxes, investment management fees, and the timing of deposits and withdrawals. Most people invest in the market over time and pull money out over time rather than investing one lump sum and leaving it there for 70 years. Many people also sell their stocks after the market drops, out of fear of losing more money, and reinvest in stocks after the market recovers, out of fear of missing out on an opportunity. This study reveals that due to these and other factors, although the average annual rate of return for the S&P 500 (U.S. large stock index) was 8.2% from January 1, 1990 to December 31, 2009, the average stock fund investor earned only 3.2% over that same 20-year period.[21]

In other words, even though a 12% average annual rate of return over a 70-year period might be mathematically accurate, the average human being would likely experience a much lower rate of return over that same time period. As discussed in Chapter Two, sometimes we are tricked into thinking that money works the same as math, but it does not.

This is why I recommend taking a balanced approach and being well-diversified, not just in stocks, but also among other asset classes. If you knew your stock investments were going to yield you only a 3% annualized return after twenty years of losing sleep every day the market goes down, wouldn't you rather have kept it all in a CD earning 3%, thus becoming totally immune to every apocalyptic news flash?

I am not suggesting that CDs are the solution. I personally own stocks, too, because I believe that if we do it right, hopefully we will be able to earn much more than 3% per year over time. The point is that we must have realistic expectations for what our investments can really do for us, and not depend on a 12% or even 8% return. If we are planning on a 5-6% long-term average rate of return but then succeed in earning 8%, we will be so much better off than if we had planned on 8%.

Furthermore, those who hold a significant portion of their assets in stable or guaranteed investments have the freedom to be less concerned about day-to-day market swings, or even big market crashes. Ironically, those who truly are well-diversified might also end up averaging a higher return in their stock portfolios over time than those who are completely dependent on stock market performance, because they will have the courage to leave it in the market when stock prices fall, and the flexibility to wait until it goes back up before pulling anything out. Even if they have already retired, when markets fall they can take money from safe, guaranteed assets until the market recovers so they are never forced to sell their stocks at deeply depressed prices to pay their bills. Often the conservative, balanced investor enjoys a much higher total return over time than the impatient risk-taker who constantly jumps from one hot new investment to the next. Slow and steady wins the race. Never forget Warren Buffet's Rule No. 1: Never lose money.

Beware of Shortcuts

Some people dream of obtaining financial security all in one day by winning the lottery or through investing in penny stocks.

The chances of success by either means are extremely low. The odds of winning the lottery are about 1 in 13,000,000 for single-state lotteries, and 1 in 175,000,000 for multiple-state lotteries. Yet many Americans still believe that their best chance of becoming financially secure is by winning the lottery.

Hoping for overnight success is not an acceptable strategy. I want to be 100% certain that my family will always be financially secure, and I want my clients to enjoy the same level of certainty. This is attainable by implementing the timeless principles of financial security we have been discussing.

Even if we did win the lottery or make it big overnight investing in penny stocks, it is not likely to bring lasting financial security or happiness. Many people who win the lottery end up completely broke within a few years, divorced, friendless, and sometimes even commit suicide, because they cannot handle the publicity or permissiveness that such a large sum of money received so quickly has granted them.

In 2002, Jack Whittaker won the Powerball multi-state lottery jackpot of $315,000,000. Pretty lucky guy, huh? Then why does he say that he regrets winning the lottery? Although he was very generous with his windfall for a while, he was continually bombarded with additional requests for money everywhere he went, and was sued by hundreds of people who were trying to get a piece of the pie. He lost many friends and started drinking heavily to console himself, which led to even further alienation by his community.

His greatest joy was his 17-year-old granddaughter, so he gave her four new cars and about $2,000 per week. She used much of this money for drugs, and eventually was found dead behind a junked van. Jack Whittaker is convinced that if he had not won the lottery, this would not have happened to her. He says he does not like who he has become, and that winning the lottery has ruined his life.[22]

How can winning the lottery be so detrimental? This phenomenon proves an important point. If we cannot learn to take responsibility for our own well-being and consistently put our money to best use, we will never be able to maintain financial security, regardless of how much money we receive. We must always exercise prudence and keep our wants in check. We must also be generous with others, but find ways to give that do not absolve them of personal responsibility or train them to expect a hand-out, so that they do not fall into the same debilitating trap that lottery winners do.

We can find great safety in living these principles and great joy in sacrificing to build something. I love the feeling when I reach the top of a very tall mountain after hiking for a few days. I have often contemplated how much less glorious the view at the top would appear if I had just been dropped off by helicopter because I would not have earned it through the hard work, patience, and determination that hiking requires. Likewise, we should find joy in the journey towards financial security and stop trying to get rich overnight for two major reasons:

1.   Most of us will never become rich overnight, so we need to stop daydreaming, stop wasting our precious resources on big bets that are not likely to work out, and focus on obtaining financial security in a way that is attainable.

2.   Those of us who do become rich overnight will truly have been robbed, because we will have missed out on the character building and sense of satisfaction that comes from getting there gradually through discipline and sacrifice.

Never Too Late to Start

I always chuckle when I see charts designed to scare people into investing as much as possible as soon as possible. Typically they say something like, "If you invest $5,000 a year starting at age 16 in an IRA earning 8% per year, then by age 65 your IRA will have grown to $2,863,851. However, if you wait until age 25 to start, it will only grow to $1,398,905. If you don't start until age 35, it will only grow to $611,729 at age 65, with the same $5,000 per year savings and 8% average annual return."

The reason I laugh when I see these figures is that although they are mathematically true, who has $5,000 a year to invest at age 16, unless their parents put it in for them? Furthermore, even if they could invest $5,000 a year in an IRA, wouldn't the money be better allocated towards college savings so they can maximize their future earning potential and invest much more money later?

Of course all of us would be much better off financially if we had been taught the proper cash flow hierarchy and were disciplined enough to live by it perfectly from the day we were born, but that is not reality. Crying over spilled milk is totally useless. Once we have learned what to do, we should simply get on the right path as quickly as possible, regardless of the stage of life we are in.

What about people who are close to retirement age, with very few assets and a mountain of debt? Should they even try? Yes, of course! Some people may be too far behind to ever be able to completely retire with their current lifestyle, but they could at least preserve their freedom and dignity to a certain extent by obtaining adequate protection, saving up enough for large unexpected expenses, and getting out of debt so they can live more comfortably on whatever income they might receive from Social Security or a modest pension if they were ever forced into retirement due to poor health or a layoff.

Any effort we make to adopt these principles will greatly benefit us, regardless of our current age and situation. Once we have learned them, we would be wise to begin practicing them immediately.

7

Enjoy Most of It Now

The Ultimate Lifestyle

After we have taken care of our taxes, tithing, protection, and asset building, we are free to spend the rest of our money on whatever we want, without guilt or worry. Money is meant to be spent. Spending is a lot more enjoyable when we know that we have adequate protection and assets that will always allow us to continue spending, even if things do not turn out the way we expected.

When you picture the ultimate lifestyle, what images come to mind? Do you envision yourself owning a mansion in an elite community, a cabin in the mountains, a beach house, and luxury automobiles? Do you imagine sporting the most expensive designer clothing and jewelry while dining at the finest restaurants every night?

Yes, a great lifestyle might include all of these things, but they often come at a steep price, not just in terms of money. Would your picture of the ultimate lifestyle also include the flexibility to spend lots of time with family and close friends? What about the freedom to take a vacation at the spur of the moment, the opportunity to quit a job that you really hate, or maybe even just the privilege of sleeping peacefully every night?

If we become too obsessed with working extra long hours so we can buy more items we think are essential to living a great lifestyle, we could find ourselves with a whole bunch of style and no life. Many people who have worked very hard to acquire a lot of possessions have discovered that they do not really own their things, but rather their things own them. The more we buy, the more time, energy, and money we have to spend storing it, protecting it, maintaining it, cleaning it, insuring it, and making loan payments on it. After all that, do we have any time or energy left to actually enjoy using it? If we can control our wants, we will avoid getting trapped in the rat race of earning more just to be able to waste more.

Addiction to Overspending

Although spending money is usually a positive thing, it can become a negative thing if it gets out of hand. Can overspending even become an addiction, just like overeating, gambling, or the abuse of alcohol or drugs? Absolutely. Since buying new things is so fun, shopping can evolve into a form of escapism from the hard realities of life and make us feel like we are richer than we really are.

Men may argue here that they have never had a positive shopping experience in their life. I hate shopping, too—just ask my wife. But I must admit I do like getting all the new things she brings home for me. Since this is generally an enjoyable experience, we may find it difficult to stop overspending until we fully realize the true cost of our indulgence.

Every addictive behavior results in an immediate positive payoff, although typically short-lived. If there were no positive payoff, no one would ever engage in the destructive behavior. The problem is that the pleasure wears off quickly, and then the negative consequences set in, which tend to be far more impactful and long-lasting than the initial fleeting reward.

In the case of overeating, the long-term consequences may be obesity or heart attacks. Gambling eventually results in lost wealth or increased debt. Alcohol or drug abuse may cause cognitive impairment, the loss of a job, loss of friends and family, or maybe even loss of life. Overspending may result in a loss of self-esteem, loss of freedom, strained relationships, and a whole host of other problems, as we discussed in Chapter One.

The first step to overcoming any addiction is being honest with ourselves about what it is costing us. When we realize that the cost far exceeds the benefit, the addiction becomes easier to overcome. What are we giving up when we overspend? Are all those expensive vacations really worth giving up the opportunity to buy our dream home? Is buying a brand new car every other year really worth postponing retirement for five years? Is going out to eat every night really worth not having the freedom to quit our job and start a new business?

With my wife Andrea's permission, I share a personal example that perfectly illustrates this point. One of her favorite things to spend money on is new clothes for our family. I am glad she enjoys shopping because without her I probably would have been wearing the same shirts for the past ten years!

For a while she was not keeping track of how much she was spending in this area, but a few years ago she asked me to start tracking it for her. At the end of that year she was shocked to see how much she had spent on clothing throughout the year. It was several thousand dollars more than what she thought possible. She could not believe what all those little purchases added up to over time. It made her sick to think of all the other things she could have done with that money, which she would rather have bought if she realized how much she had been spending on clothing.

Even though she still loves buying new clothes, she decided from that point forward to dramatically cut her spending in that area and redirect it towards other things she wants even more. She was able to overcome her addiction to overspending on clothing because she realized how many other more important things she was giving up for it.

Good Things Come to Those Who Wait

In the late 1960s, a psychology professor at Stanford University named Walter Mischel conducted an experiment on 653 preschool-aged children to measure their ability to delay gratification. First a researcher would give them a small treat, such as a marshmallow or a cookie. Then he would tell them that he was going to step out for a few minutes, and if they did not eat the treat until he returned, he would give them another one.

Most of the children ate the treat right away or were only able to wait a few minutes. Only 30% of them were able to wait the full 15 minutes until the researcher returned. The disciplined children employed several techniques to help them resist the temptation to eat the treat, such as covering their eyes, looking under the table, walking around, and singing songs.

Over the years, Professor Mischel conducted additional experiments on these same children, and was surprised to discover that later in life those who had been the quickest to eat the treat in the original experiment tended to have more behavioral problems, fewer friends, lower test scores, and were more overweight than those who were able to wait longer.[23]

What long-term financial benefits might we reap by disciplining ourselves to wait a little bit longer for what we want now? Keeping a clear perspective on this issue can be very difficult because we live in a society that demands everything now. The word "patience" has practically been deleted from our vocabulary. We enjoy instant access to information, books, pictures, movies, and music at the click of a mouse. We can buy just about any kind of food we want at any time of the year, any time of day or night. We are bombarded with offers to buy now and pay later. Why should we have to wait for anything? Is patience an antiquated principle that is no longer applicable to our modern society?

The problem is that instant gratification, even when easily accessible, usually comes at a hefty price. Items purchased at a convenience store typically cost much more than they would at a regular grocery store. Fast food in excess drains our wallets and robs our health. When we make purchases on credit, we often end up paying way more over time than we would have paid if we had saved up to buy with cash. When we buy impulsively we often spend way more than we would have if we had shopped around a little or spent a little more time contemplating whether we really even wanted it. The inability to delay gratification not only threatens our financial security, but also threatens to destroy our most meaningful relationships, our health, and our self-esteem.

On the other hand, great satisfaction comes from waiting patiently for and working hard to acquire something we want. One year we decided to save up for a special family vacation that would take place a year later. Of course we already had enough money to pay for the vacation right away, but we did not want to take it from our savings accounts that were intended for other purposes. We also thought it would be a great learning experience for our daughters, ages five and six at the time, to contribute to our efforts to save for the trip.

It was very touching to see that every time they received a little money from birthday or Christmas gifts, from the Tooth Fairy, or from doing chores, they would put all of it in the "vacation fund jar." At first I felt guilty allowing them to put in every penny they received because the tiny amounts they gave were such a huge sacrifice for them, yet contributed so insignificantly to the total amount we would need. However, I realized that this exercise was teaching them an important principle. Every time they contributed, their excitement for the vacation grew.

We saved up enough money for the vacation right on schedule, and had a fabulous time. It was everything we dreamed it would be. We all felt a great sense of accomplishment knowing that our hard work, patience, and sacrifice paid off.

Then an interesting thing happened. A few months later, a family member surprised us with an offer to take our whole family back to the same destination, all expenses paid. Before we knew it, we were back at the same spot.

It felt strange to be back there so soon, without any of the sacrifice or prolonged anticipation we had experienced before. We still had fun, and were very grateful to this family member for providing the opportunity, but we marveled at how much less exciting the trip was the second time. Since we did not have to work for it or wait patiently for our dream to be realized, the second trip was much less rewarding for us, and in a way we felt robbed.

So it is with anything we work patiently to acquire. We receive the greatest satisfaction from the things for which we work the hardest. The most rewarding things in life cannot be attained in an instant. A high-quality education, a successful career, lasting friendships, physical fitness, and a lifetime of financial security all require patience, hard work, and sacrifice.

As we patiently seek to acquire lasting financial security, we would be wise to emulate the example of the disciplined children from Professor Mischel's experiment by employing techniques that will help us avoid the temptation to overspend. Such techniques might include not carrying around credit cards or excessive amounts of cash, minimizing our window shopping, limiting our involvement with people who pressure us to spend beyond our means, and carefully planning how we will spend our money.

Creating a Spending Plan

Whether they make a lot of money or squeak by on a meager salary, most people shiver when they hear the word "budget." Since the "B word" typically evokes such negative emotions, I prefer to call it a Spending Plan. I enjoy thinking about how I am going to spend my money much more than I enjoy contemplating how to restrict myself by living within a budget. After all, money is ultimately meant to be spent, right?

Creating a spending plan is a beautiful thing because it is the only way to ensure that our money will go to the things we want most, not just to the things we want now. As we discussed in Chapter One, this is a critical distinction, because the two are often mutually exclusive. We can never have enough money to buy everything we want.

Therefore, we should think of our spending plan as a friend who helps us get what we want most, not as an enemy to all happiness. If we have already allocated the proper amounts to taxes, tithing, insurance, and savings, then we are most of the way there. In fact, we do not even have to keep track of where the rest of it goes if we do not want to. The most important thing is to distinguish between fixed, totally necessary expenses (such as mortgage payments and utilities) and discretionary expenses (such as eating out and taking vacations). We must be sure we have enough to cover the fixed expenses first, and then we can spend whatever is left on the extras.

In our family, as we have learned to discipline ourselves we have realized that sticking to our spending plan actually feels more liberating than restrictive. Our diligence has resulted in the freedom to buy a bigger house, take better vacations, save more for the future, and more aggressively pay down debts. It also feels very satisfying, even sanctifying, to make personal sacrifices in order to consistently live within our predetermined spending plan. We feel much more powerful and at peace about our future than we felt before.

Believe it or not, sometimes it can even be kind of fun to make everything work within the plan, almost like a game. This came as a surprise to me, but the more I thought about it, the more sense it made because rules and boundaries are the essence of any game. How much fun would it be to play football without any rules or boundaries? How exciting would it be to play a video game with unlimited lives, unlimited ammunition, and no time limit? The boundaries are what make any game interesting and meaningful, including the game of money management.

The first step to creating a realistic spending plan is to track what we are currently spending. When we start keeping track, our spending will automatically go down because we will be more aware of where it is all going. Ideally we would analyze the past year's worth of spending to come up with some meaningful goals, but I would recommend reviewing at least the past three months.

Keep in mind that although some regular expenses may occur only on a quarterly or annual basis, they should still be included in the spending plan. Also remember that some expenses, such as utilities, may vary widely depending on the season. That is why a twelve-month record would be the most accurate. We must not make it too complicated, though, or we will never get it done. Modern technology makes this process much easier than it used to be. We might even be able to just download our spending history from our online banking.

When labeling purchases, be sure not to create too many categories. Broad categories will give a clearer sense of what is really happening, and will be less cumbersome to keep track of over time.

The following six broad categories are the essentials I would recommend closely tracking:

1. Taxes
2. Charity
3. Insurance
4. Savings
5. Fixed Spending
6. Discretionary Spending

Here I have listed sample subcategories to give a clearer picture of what might be included in each broad category:

1. Taxes
    a. Federal income taxes
    b. Social Security and Medicare taxes
    c. State and local income taxes
    d. Property taxes
2. Charity
    a. Tithing
    b. Other charitable donations
3. Insurance
    a. Auto insurance
    b. Homeowners insurance
    c. Umbrella liability insurance
    d. Medical insurance
    e. Disability insurance
    f. Long term care insurance
    g. Term life insurance (not whole life)
4. Savings
    a. Contributions to savings and investment accounts which we are not planning to spend in the near future
    b. Contributions to retirement accounts
    c. Whole life insurance premiums
    d. Mortgage payments for real estate property that we do not personally occupy
    e. Investments in business interests

5. Fixed Spending (expenses that are the same every month or over which we have very little control)
    a. Mortgage payments
    b. Other debt payments
    c. Utilities, cable, internet, phone
    d. Automobile fuel and maintenance
    e. Household services such as cleaning, landscaping, pest control, and pool service
    f. Education expenses (private school, college tuition, books, subscriptions, athletic training, music lessons, dance lessons, etc.)
6. Discretionary Spending (expenses that are non-essential or more easily controlled)
    a. Groceries (although essential, can be controlled somewhat by our choice of products and vendors)
    b. Clothing
    c. Dining out
    d. Entertainment
    e. Vacations
    f. Gifts
    g. Furniture and household décor
    h. Home improvement

I strongly recommend setting up two separate checking accounts to help control spending. This makes living by the spending plan a cinch because we can use the primary checking account to cover the first five categories and the secondary account to cover all discretionary spending. With this system, all income is originally deposited into the primary checking account. Then at the beginning of each month we calculate how much we will need for the first five categories and transfer whatever is left over to the discretionary account. We can spend our discretionary account all the way down to zero each month if we want to, without worrying about robbing from the essentials. At any time we can look up our discretionary account balance online to see how much more we can spend on fun things that month, without having to track how much we spent so far. At the beginning of the next month we simply repeat the process, making adjustments as needed.

My wife Andrea and I have been using this method for a while, and it works great. We both love it because it gives her complete control over all discretionary items without wondering how much she can afford to spend each month. Before we used this system I felt like she was always coming to me for "permission" to buy every little thing because she never knew exactly where we stood financially. Sometimes this resulted in resentment because we would often disagree on how much should be spent on certain things.

I tried to get her to handle all of our personal finances to avoid this situation, but she hated doing it. This new system has been great for our marriage because now I don't have to agree with or even know about how much she spends on specific items because she always does a great job staying within the amount we have allocated to discretionary spending. She really enjoys being able to choose what to buy because if she wants to spend a little less on groceries or eating out one month, she can splurge on something else without having to ask whether we can afford it.

Those who do not like using debit cards or checks may consider withdrawing a certain amount of cash at the beginning of each month to cover discretionary spending instead of setting up a separate checking account. Once the cash is gone, all discretionary spending should stop until the beginning of the next month.

Some people prefer to use credit cards for everything so they can rack up as many rewards points as possible. However, I have observed that most people find it much more difficult to control discretionary spending when using credit cards because they don't realize how much they have spent until they get the huge bill at the end of the month. Using debit cards or cash clarifies how much money we have left in our spending plan for the month. The ability to stay within a predetermined amount of discretionary spending that fits our overall priorities is much more valuable than any credit card rewards could ever be.

Once we are committed to a spending plan, it can be fun to see how far we can stretch our discretionary account by looking for great deals. Sometimes I am amazed by how much more we can get for our money when buying deeply discounted or quality used items. However, we must be careful not to be penny wise and pound foolish. We may be tempted to buy lots of things we see that we don't really need when searching for a "great deal" on something we do need. Stay on task when shopping.

What about the amount of time required to find these deals? We may unwittingly spend hours researching the best deal, especially online, when in the end we might only save $10 or find a marginal improvement in quality. The amount of time we spend researching the best deal should be proportionate to the cost of the item.

Many people spend hours clipping coupons and bouncing around from store to store to save a few dollars, yet pay thousands more than necessary in insurance premiums, taxes, or investment fees every year because they "don't have time" to meet with a financial planner who can help them optimize these costs. We should never underestimate the value of our time. Time is money, so we must treat it with just as much respect, if not more.

Don't Allow Others to Dictate Your Spending

How do we decide how much money to spend on each purchase? Most people do not seem to give it much thought. If a bank will loan them the money, they buy it whether they can really afford it or not.

Several years ago I met a married couple who were barely making ends meet on the husband's modest income. The wife also worked full-time, but the majority of her paycheck went to the monthly payment of a three-year lease on a high-end Mercedes-Benz. I was amazed that she was willing to work so hard for nothing more than a glamorous image on the road, with nothing to show for it when she would have to give the car back to the dealership in a short three years.

This is one small example of how powerful our desire to "keep up with the Joneses" can be. How often do we indirectly allow friends, acquaintances, or even strangers dictate our spending because of the pressure we feel to maintain a certain image around them? How good are we at taking spending advice only from people who are financially secure? Anyone who would ridicule us for not being willing to blow money on extravagant luxuries we cannot afford is probably just a step away from bankruptcy himself.

How do we decide how big of a house to buy? Many people let the banks decide for them by acquiring the largest mortgage for which they can qualify. Did you know that some banks allow people to qualify for a mortgage payment of up to 35% of their gross monthly income?

Banks do not care about our long-term financial security. They do not care if we cannot afford to save for the future because our mortgage payment takes up too much of our income. All they care about is whether we can consistently make our mortgage payment so they can make as much money on us as possible. If we are serious about being financially secure for life, our mortgage payment should be no more than 15% of our gross monthly income. Less than 15% is even better.

How do we decide how much to spend on Christmas and other gifts? Do we give out of love, out of obligation, or for show? We tend to worry way too much about what others will think about what we give, when we should be focusing more on what would be meaningful gifts that we can afford. Are we truly giving for the benefit of others, or are we giving to portray an image of success and generosity?

Spending too much on gifts is easy because we may feel like we are being selfish if we fail to give the same quality or quantity of gifts that the Joneses were able to give by incurring large amounts of debt. Of course we should give generously, but we cannot give that which is not ours to begin with. The amount we spend on gifts should always stay within our spending plan. If we must make sacrifices in other areas to give nice gifts while staying within our means, doesn't that make it more of a true gift anyway?

Include Your Spouse in Spending Decisions

The only person who should have a strong influence on our spending decisions is our spouse. Marriage is an equal partnership, not a dictatorship where one spouse rules over the other. I have seen some families where the husband dictates all spending decisions and others where the wife does. Neither is healthy.

It is normal for one spouse to primarily handle the day-to-day financial affairs such as shopping, paying bills, or tracking expenses, but that is not what I am talking about. We should make the important decisions together, such as how much money to save each month or how big of a mortgage to get. Both spouses should have an equal say on large purchases.

Unselfishness and compromise will likely be necessary for both parties to come to a mutual agreement. We each have unique interests, tastes, talents, priorities, attitudes, backgrounds, perspectives, experiences, fears, and dreams, so we must understand and respect that of our spouse. Part of the benefit of marriage is that our differences often balance each other out so together we have a healthier outlook on life and become greater than the sum of our parts.

Permission to Spend a Lot of Money

Spending a lot of money on big houses, luxury cars, or expensive vacations is okay if we can afford them and if we are generous with what we have. I used to think it was bad to spend a ton of money on these items because of how much good could be done for other people with that money instead. However, I now realize that I was wrong to feel that way.

Over the years I have come to know a lot of very humble, incredibly generous people who also live a fairly lavish lifestyle. Many successful people I know have made huge sacrifices and worked very hard to build their wealth, carry very little debt or none at all, and are very generous with their time, abilities, and money to help other people. Why shouldn't they be able to buy nice things for themselves if they can afford them and still give generously to others who are less fortunate?

We must not judge one another in these matters. A poor person who thinks someone is selfish for driving an expensive car is just as much in the wrong as a rich person who thinks someone is inferior for driving an old clunker.

Acceptable Forms of Personal Debt

Although I have been harsh on debt throughout this book and believe we should pay cash for as many things as possible, I acknowledge that some forms of debt may be the best way to meet some of our most critical spending needs. When used wisely and sparingly, it can provide tremendous opportunities for economic improvement that may never be available otherwise.

In my opinion, the most responsible use of personal debt would be limited to reasonable amounts for education, a modest home, and basic transportation. It may also be prudent for businesses to incur certain forms of debt at sensible levels for expansion that would be impossible otherwise, but we will limit our discussion here to personal debt.

Why am I okay with debt for these purposes? Since higher education often dramatically improves potential earning power, and since our ability to earn an income is typically our greatest asset throughout most of our life, student loans may produce a higher long-term return than any other investment we could make. If a student's parents or grandparents cannot afford to pay higher education costs for her, she may never be able to save up enough money on her own to pay for the schooling required to increase her earning power so substantially. In this case, student loans can be a very valuable tool.

Still, we must be careful not to spend more on education than we can reasonably expect to be able to pay back based on the earning potential of employment opportunities related to our field of study. We can minimize the use of student loans by seeking to qualify for as many scholarships and grants as possible and by working part-time. We should also remember that paying exorbitant tuition expenses for the most prestigious schools will not necessarily result in significantly higher earning potential than we could attain from lower-cost alternatives.

Financing the purchase of a modest home can be a smart move if the monthly mortgage payments are comparable to what we would be paying to rent a similar place because over time rents may increase, but mortgage payments normally stay the same and eventually become paid off. We can also participate in any potential appreciation of the value of the home.

However, we must be careful not to bite off more than we can chew, as I mentioned earlier. We should keep our mortgage payment within 15% of our gross income. We should also shy away from purchasing a home if we are only planning to stay in it for a short time because short-term real estate prices can be very unpredictable. If only staying somewhere for a short time, renting is a much better solution because of its flexibility and the avoidance of other expenses associated with home ownership, such as property taxes, insurance, maintenance, and repairs.

We may need our own car to be able to earn an income, even if we cannot afford to pay cash for it at first. Renting a car for an extended period would be way too expensive, so it might be best to buy our own car on credit, as long as we get a reasonable interest rate and do not pay too much for it. Even though we may want a brand new Lexus right away, it would be better to start with something less expensive just to get us to work, then save up to buy a Lexus later.

Everything else we buy ideally would be paid for with cash. Those who live by this rule find themselves much happier, less stressed, and less susceptible to all of the inevitable unexpected events that are a normal part of life.

Render to Every Man His Due

Those of us who have already acquired excessive amounts of debt must do all within our power to pay it back. The Lord said, "And as ye would that men should do to you, do ye also to them likewise" (Luke 6:31). When you loan someone money, do you want to be repaid? When you provide a professional service, do you expect to be fairly compensated? We should treat others, even faceless financial institutions, as we would want to be treated when it comes to financial obligations.

Some people believe that if they can finagle a way to pay less than they originally agreed to pay, or if they can avoid paying altogether, it is a manifestation of their superior intellect. In reality it is often nothing more than a selfish demonstration of their disregard for others that diminishes their character. Such conduct may provide some short-term gains, but the long-term consequences can be severe. Failing to meet our obligations often results in damaged relationships, loss of trust, seared conscience, loss of self-respect, bad credit, and maybe even imprisonment. In the words of the great Psalmist, "The wicked borroweth, and payeth not again: but the righteous sheweth mercy, and giveth" (Psalms 37:21).

Not only should we meet all of our obligations, but we should also pay them on time. Not doing so is a form of dishonesty and disrespect. Doing so avoids unnecessary late fees or higher interest charges and helps us maintain good credit, which can result in lower interest rates, lower insurance premiums, and maybe even better employment.

Of course it may take us longer at times to repay our debts than we originally agreed to, through no fault of our own. Sometimes even bankruptcy may be unavoidable. Creditors should be merciful to those who in good faith truly cannot repay. However, I have seen many people legally erase mountains of debt simply because it was the easiest way out, not because they could not afford to repay. This is unfair to their creditors, to society, and to themselves.

It may not be fun to repay our debts. It may require working longer hours or waiting for a long time to purchase things we really want. This is not a bad thing. Making such sacrifices to repay our debts will help us feel much better about ourselves and will motivate us to be more cautious with our purchases in the future.

Attitude of Gratitude

One of the best ways to gain the discipline to live within our means and stick to our spending plan is to cultivate an attitude of gratitude. When we are more aware of and grateful for the rich abundance with which we have already been blessed, we become less concerned about the few things we lack. We become less interested in the Joneses' possessions or attitudes towards us and more fully enjoy that which we already have.

Whenever we feel frustrated that we cannot have something we really want, we should write a list of all the wonderful things we already have. By the time we get to the end of the first page, most of us would probably realize that we do not really need whatever it was that we wanted so badly. If we continued writing we could probably come up with another ten pages.

When we live joyfully within our means after taking care of our taxes, tithing, protection, and savings, we will more fully enjoy the things we can buy with whatever is left over. We will also be at peace knowing we are likely to be able to continue enjoying our possessions for a long time, regardless of whatever unexpected events might be thrown our way.

8

Work by Choice

Why Do We Work?

For most of us, work is necessary for survival. We must earn money to buy the things we need and want. Some people love to work. Others wish they never had to work another day of their lives. What connotation does the word "work" have for you?

David O. McKay counseled, "Let us realize that the privilege to work is a gift, that power to work is a blessing, that love of work is success." Due to the massive layoffs and slow job recovery of the recent Great Recession, many who always thought they hated working have discovered that David O. McKay was right. They long for the privilege of working again after experiencing the pains of long-term unemployment.

What are the pains of unemployment? Of course the financial consequences can be devastating, but that is not all. People who have lost the opportunity to work for an extended period come to realize that working also yields significant psychological, emotional, intellectual, social, physical, and spiritual benefits. When we stop working, we tend to feel less valuable and less confident in ourselves. Our minds and our bodies weaken. We become less socially engaging.

Lasting happiness and growth can only come from continually working to improve our lives and the lives of other people. King Solomon taught, "The sleep of a labouring man is sweet, whether he eat little or much: but the abundance of the rich will not suffer him to sleep" (Ecclesiastes 5:12).

I have found this to be true. I never feel better than at the end of an exceptionally hard day's work. Honest toil is the best cure for insomnia, especially when physical labor is involved.

On the other hand, at the end of a long vacation I always feel sluggish and anxious to get back to work. Of course appropriate amounts and types of recreation bring us joy and improve our productivity when we return to our work. However, the pursuit of nonstop leisure for years and years cannot reap satisfaction. To be happy, we must find proper balance between work and play throughout our lives.

Just before Adam and Eve were cast out of the Garden of Eden, God instructed, "Cursed is the ground for thy sake; in sorrow shalt thou eat of it all the days of thy life; thorns also and thistles shall it bring forth to thee…In the sweat of thy face shalt thou eat bread, till thou return unto the ground…" (Genesis 3:17-19). "For thy sake" means "for your benefit." God knew that Adam and Eve would benefit from having to work hard for their food throughout their entire lives. Therefore, he purposely made growing food difficult by providing thorns, thistles, and many other obstacles.

As children of Adam and Eve, we all have inherited the same mandate. We are very fortunate to live in a time when we do not have to work as hard as they did to produce our own food, clothing, or shelter, thanks to modern technology, specialization, and global trade. However, work will always be a spiritual necessity for all of us, even when it is not a financial necessity.

What do I mean by "work?" Of course I am not suggesting that everyone needs to maintain a full-time career to reap the benefits of labor. Many kinds of work that do not pay are just as stimulating.

The Merriam-Webster Dictionary defines work as "activity in which one exerts strength or faculties to do or perform something; sustained physical or mental effort to overcome obstacles and achieve an objective or result." The benefits of working stem from the effort required to overcome an obstacle. The more difficult the work is, the more rewarding the outcome.

Which is more rewarding, a walk around the block, or a hike to the peak of a tall mountain? What good is a workout at the gym without weights? Resistance is what builds muscle and produces the sense of accomplishment and post-workout high.

Conversely, when we stop using our muscles, they weaken and shrink over time. Our intellectual, social, and spiritual "muscles" also atrophy if we do not regularly exercise them. We must always work, no matter the type, as long as it is challenging and does some good in the world.

Why Are We Trying to Stop Working?

We live in a society that glorifies a life of ease. We are conditioned to long for the day when every hour can be filled with golfing, shopping, or lying on the beach. Some of us hate our jobs so badly that we just go through the motions, counting down the days until retirement. We aspire to quit our jobs and do all the things we have always dreamed of doing but never had time to do because we were too busy working.

Most people assume that they will end their careers at age 65 and then kick back for the rest of their lives. After all, isn't this is the predetermined destiny of every American?

Our life's plan is completely laid out for us by the federal government. We go to elementary school at a certain age, then junior high, then high school. When we graduate from high school, we either go to college or start working. Throughout our schooling and our careers we learn to dread Mondays and love Fridays. Then at age 65 we "graduate" from working.

Is retirement really that automatic? Do we have a constitutional right to stop working on our 65th birthday? Where does this notion come from?

Well, for a long time, that was the age at which we could start taking our full Social Security retirement benefits. Also, many companies have instituted the practice of retiring their employees at age 65 in order to replace them with less expensive younger workers. These and other factors have contributed to a collective cultural belief that it is our destiny to retire at age 65, regardless of our personal level of financial preparation for it.

Retirement is a privilege, not a right. Since most people now approaching that magical age have not saved enough, owe too much debt, or have taken too much risk with their investments, most of them will probably never be able to completely stop working unless they dramatically reduce their lifestyle or move in with their kids. We tend to underestimate how much money it would take to retire comfortably for the rest of our lives. Not very many people succeed at generating enough investment income to completely replace the amount of income they could earn by working.

As disappointing as that may sound, an even more critical issue is at stake. Even those who can afford to retire with a great lifestyle may discover that completely shutting off work does not turn out to be the paradise they always dreamed it would be. Many people who cease all forms of meaningful work sink into depression because they are no longer producing anything of value to anyone and have cut off important social connections.

A man I know complains that his ex-partner who has retired still hangs out in the office several times a week just to chat and see what is going on with the company. He doesn't know what to do with himself since he stopped working. The company was his life for so long that he simply cannot shut it off.

For a while the partner who still runs the company was debating whether he should also retire because it is a very stressful and volatile business. I responded, "I guess you just need to ask yourself, how much is enough?" He already had saved up several million dollars in liquid assets at the time, had no debt, and lived a very conservative lifestyle. He responded, "That's not the point. I agree that I could afford to retire right now if I sold the company, but then what would I do? I love my life right now because every day I wake up not knowing what new challenge I am going to have to overcome. This company gives me a reason to get out of bed in the morning and keeps me alive."

Many retirees lose their identity, become lonely, and start to feel that their existence has no purpose. They often grow in their criticism of others and in their obsession over petty things that did not bother them before because they were too busy working. For these and other reasons, many marriages are destroyed in retirement and some retirees even become suicidal.

What did the Lord teach about the retirement mentality? Consider how the following parable from the Bible might relate to this topic: "And he spake a parable unto them, saying, The ground of a certain rich man brought forth plentifully: And he thought within himself, saying, What shall I do, because I have no room where to bestow my fruits? And he said, This will I do: I will pull down my barns, and build greater; and there will I bestow all my fruits and my goods. And I will say to my soul, Soul, thou hast much goods laid up for many years; take thine ease, eat, drink, and be merry. But God said unto him, Thou fool, this night thy soul shall be required of thee: then whose shall those things be, which thou hast provided? So is he that layeth up treasure for himself, and is not rich toward God" (Luke 12:16-21).

Don't Retire—Re-fire!

May I recommend a more inspiring vision of the final decades of life? Never completely retire! Now I am not suggesting that we need to continue working for The Man till the day we die no matter how badly we hate it. If we don't love our current job, we should start figuring out a way to transition into spending our time and energy doing more meaningful work that we enjoy—work that better capitalizes on our unique talents, training and interests. We should strive to get to a point where we work because we want to, not just because we have to.

I am saddened by the fact that so many people waste their whole career performing work they abhor in order to support an extravagant lifestyle or retire early. What is even more tragic is that many of these people inadvertently destroy family relationships because they were so stressed and busy working to create a "better life" for their family, when in reality all the family wanted was more quality time with them. Would it not be better to find joy in the journey by employing a proper balance among work, play, family time, and community or church service along the way, rather than doing nothing but work for 40 years and then nothing but play for 20 years?

Richard Nelson Bolles, author of the best-selling book *What Color is Your Parachute?*, believes that each of us has been charged with a specific mission in life, for which we have been endowed with unique talents. He asserts that each person who discovers and focuses on doing what he does best will be much more successful and of greater benefit to society than he who just takes whatever job comes along or tries to fit an unsuitable mold imposed upon him by others. We can easily detect our unique talents and skills because these are the things we enjoy doing most. The challenge is figuring out how to transfer our unique abilities into something society is willing to pay for. The exercises in Mr. Bolles's book help with that discovery process.[24]

In college I studied music composition, piano, and singing. Some of my professors were very disappointed I did not pursue a career in music because they thought I showed a lot of promise, but I knew it would be a tough gig for my family if I went that route. As I mentioned in the introduction, I did not want my wife and children to suffer financially. I also wanted to be able to spend plenty of time with them, which I knew would be difficult as a professional musician. I do not regret studying music in college because I still love to compose and perform, but I am *very* glad I decided not to rely on it for a living.

Since I chose not to pursue a music career, I had to figure out how to transfer my unique abilities into something else of value to other people. Thanks to the exercises in *What Color is Your Parachute?*, I discovered that my talents as a composer and performer could also help me be a great financial planner. Who would have thought that my attention to detail, self-motivation, ability to communicate effectively, love of working with people, ability to analyze and synthesize large amounts of data, and desire to make a positive difference in the lives of others would all be valuable traits both as a musician and as a financial planner? It is never too late to re-evaluate what might be the best use of our unique abilities and how to make money doing it.

On the other hand, we must be careful not to get too carried away with trying to find the ultimate profession. We must have realistic expectations because not everyone can fit what they enjoy doing most into a marketable skill. Working just for the sake of working, regardless of the type, brings much more satisfaction than waiting around for the perfect job. We can find fulfillment in any kind of work as long as the work is honorable.

I learned this principle selling pest control door-to-door during college. Can you think of a more detestable job? Yet it surprised me to discover how fulfilling it was to be of service to other people, to work hard to accomplish my goals, and to be able to pay all of my own college expenses without student loans, even though the work was so unglamorous. This experience also helped me realize I did not have to pursue a music career to be happy.

We must also keep in mind that the grass is not always greener on the other side. Every occupation presents its own set of challenges and frustrations. That is the nature of work. If there were no challenges, it would not require effort. If it were easy and fun all the time, it would not be work. Its less desirable aspects engender the satisfaction, sense of accomplishment, and financial reward we seek.

For thousands of years, most people did not have much choice in the type of labor they performed. Throughout history most people had to grow and prepare their own food, build their own houses, and make their own clothes. Even now, many people throughout the world must engage in menial tasks and hard physical labor for very long hours every day just to provide the basic necessities of life. This is honorable work that can be very satisfying when done with the right attitude. Sometimes we just need to rediscover the fulfillment that comes from the nature of work itself, regardless of the type.

Many people who love what they do and would be happy to continue doing it forever are forced out of full-time employment or are forced to close the doors of their business due to factors outside of their control, such as economic conditions, technological changes, or personal health problems. During the Great Recession, many people have been unemployed for a long time, waiting for their old jobs to come back. Unfortunately, many of the jobs that were lost may never come back because the economy has changed so dramatically.

When necessary, we must be willing to retrain or relocate in order to provide for ourselves. If we cannot retrain or relocate, we should find creative ways to continue bringing value to others. We can teach, consult, start our own business, or serve in our church or community. I admire those who promptly make whatever adjustments are necessary to reclaim their status as productive members of society.

We should seek to obtain as much education as possible throughout our lives in order to continually expand our value to other people, our competitive edge, and our potential earning power. Thus, when the winds of change blow the economy in a new direction, we will be better equipped to adapt.

The key is to be a producer throughout life, never just a consumer. Working in some capacity throughout our lives, even after retiring from our normal jobs, will not only reap tremendous financial benefits, but also bring fulfillment and improve our physical, emotional, mental, and spiritual health. We will more easily preserve our self-esteem and our marriages because we will continue to be a benefit to others. We will also be a great example to our children, grandchildren, and others who may depend on us to teach them the importance of cultivating a strong work ethic and a love for work.

Mark Victor Hansen and Art Linkletter wrote a fascinating book on this subject entitled *How to Make the Rest of Your Life the Best of Your Life*. In this book the renowned psychologist and gerontologist Dr. Ken Dychtwald points out that the modern notion of retirement in our country is partially a fruit of the industrial era, when we started to view the vibrancy of youth as being more valuable than the wisdom of maturity. Then during the Great Depression, President Roosevelt was faced with a 25% unemployment rate. Many of the unemployed were young and single, afraid to marry and have children because their future was so uncertain. In the words of Dr. Dychtwald, "What struck [Roosevelt] was that if he could somehow remove some people from the workforce, he could make room for the young. So he made a thoughtful and probably sensible decision: he institutionalized old age and retirement and formalized the notion that older people were no longer able to make a contribution.

"Life expectancy the day that Social Security was passed was only sixty-three. There were forty workers for each recipient, and so there wasn't a sensitivity that there'd be a strain on the economy from the small number of anticipated retirees. A little-known fact is that for the fifteen years after Social Security was passed, the average age at which people retired was seventy. Even though people were told that they should step out the door, the elders back then resisted. Why? Because they wanted to earn a living. They felt good about the contributions they made, and they thought, 'Well, what am I going to do if I sit at home all the time?'"

He goes on to explain that as more and more retirees started collecting Social Security benefits, we began to believe as a society that we are all entitled to retire and that other people should help pay for it. Retirement became a symbol of the ultimate stage of life, a much happier state than working. However, many people have observed close friends and family members who are bored out of their minds in retirement, so now we are beginning to re-evaluate what it really means.

Dr. Dichtwald observed, "I think a lot of people are scratching their heads right now and saying, 'Who do I really want to be when I'm older?' Maybe it's not a matter of either working full-time or playing full-time; maybe it's about creating a new balance between work and leisure. More time for family and leisure, but not the end of work."[25]

How Do We Get There?

Have I convinced you to plan to continue working in some capacity throughout the rest of your life? If so, great—now we need to discuss how to get to the point where you can do what you love, rather than just having to work to survive.

If I have not convinced you to continue working, that's okay, too. The next chapter applies even more specifically to you.

9

Create Secure Retirement Income

Who Can We Count on for a Secure Retirement?

Retirement is a privilege, not a right. If we ever want to be able to live a comfortable, secure retirement, we must take responsibility for making it happen ourselves. If we expect the government or our employer to provide for us forever, we may be disappointed because they are ill-equipped to do so. That's okay, because it is not their responsibility anyway.

What is the future outlook for Social Security? Have you ever read the front of your annual Social Security statement? Here is part of what it said in 2008:

> "Social Security is the largest source of income for most elderly Americans today, but Social Security was never intended to be your only source of income when you retire. You also will need other savings, investments, pensions or retirement accounts to make sure you have enough money to live comfortably when you retire...

> "Social Security is a compact between generations. For decades, America has kept the promise of security for its workers and their families. Now, however, the Social Security System is facing serious financial problems, and action is needed soon to make sure the system will be sound when today's younger workers are ready for retirement.

"In 2017 we will begin paying more in benefits than we collect in taxes. Without changes, by 2041 the Social Security Trust Fund will be exhausted and there will be enough money to pay only about 78 cents for every dollar of scheduled benefits. We need to resolve these issues soon to make sure Social Security continues to provide a foundation of protection for future generations."

Note the difference in wording for the last paragraph of the 2010 Social Security statement, only two years later:

"In *2016* we will begin paying more in benefits than we collect in taxes. Without changes, by *2037* the Social Security Trust Fund will be exhausted and there will be enough money to pay only about *76* cents for every dollar of scheduled benefits…" (emphasis added).

The federal government is not the only institution struggling to meet its obligations. Many corporate and local government pensions are also in severe financial trouble. Investment earnings and tax revenues have plummeted, while retirees dependent on these pensions are living longer than expected. Although pensions do provide substantial retirement income stability, we cannot completely rely on them if we want to ensure comfortable, secure retirement income for as long as we live.

Obtaining the freedom to do what we want without having to work, or to work fewer hours in a job that we enjoy, requires diligent preparation and personal sacrifice. The goal is to eventually have our money work for us, rather than always working for money.

For most of us, our ability to earn an income is far more valuable than all of our other assets combined. It is very difficult and usually takes a long time to get to the point where our investments can produce more income than we can earn by working. Most people never get to that point. However, those who do reach it become truly financially independent, as long as their investments continue to perform well.

For example, if someone is accustomed to making $250,000 per year in their profession, what would the value of their investments have to be to earn the same level of income? That depends on the rate of return, but if they can make 5% per year, the value of their investments must equal $5,000,000 to generate $250,000 of annual income without depleting principal.

Sounds like a piece of cake, right? It is simple, but not easy. Why is it not easy? Several powerful forces oppose our efforts. Let's unravel the most common and significant threats to enjoying a secure, comfortable retirement. Then we will discuss how to overcome them.

Threats to a Secure, Comfortable Retirement

1. Inability to Save Money

The single biggest threat to a secure retirement is the lack of discipline to save an adequate amount for the future. If we are serious about retiring, we must stop worrying about the Joneses and start putting away at least 20% of what we make—more if possible—especially if we plan to completely stop working someday.

2. Excessive Debt

As we discussed earlier, many people lock themselves into hefty long-term monthly commitments when times are good, assuming they will always be making as much as they do when they incur the debt. When unemployment, disability, or the desire to retire set in, they realize their options are very limited. Those who avoid and eliminate debt require much less income from their investments to live a comfortable lifestyle in retirement. Therefore, they are not as dependent on high investment balances or high rates of return.

3. Poor Investment Decisions

When we take too much risk with our investments in an effort to shortcut the retirement savings process, we often get burned, sometimes even so severely that we lose many years' worth of precious sacrifice. On the other hand, if we fail to earn anything on our investments, we inadvertently may be losing money every year to inflation. The key is to put our money to work so it is not just sitting idle, and to be content with modest gains.

4. Inflation

What is inflation? It is the rate at which the general cost of goods and services increases from year to year. Typically we do not feel the impact of inflation too much when we are working full-time because earned income for most people generally tends to increase by a rate comparable to the rate of inflation. However, if we stop working and depend entirely on fixed income from pensions or investments, we feel the impact of inflation very acutely because every year our fixed income is able to purchase fewer and fewer goods and services.

How big of an impact can inflation have over time? According to the U.S. Department of Labor's Bureau of Labor Statistics, which measures the Consumer Price Index (CPI), I would need about $265,000 in 2010 to buy the same goods and services I could have bought with only $100,000 in 1980.[26] That is a 3.3% average annual inflation rate, but the rate was not constant over that time period. It ranged from 13.5% to less than 0% from year to year, so the impact of inflation was greater in some years than in others. If a similar average inflation rate were to continue for another 30 years, then in 2040 it would cost me $700,000 to pay for the same goods and services I would have spent $265,000 on in 2010.

Another related challenge is that we will want or need to buy several items during retirement that are not included in our normal monthly spending now. Things wear out and need to be replaced. We may need to buy new cars, new roofs, new carpet, new appliances, and so on. Where is the money going to come from for such large purchases if we are barely squeaking by on a limited fixed monthly income?

Additionally, how many new products will we consider to be essential in the future although we cannot even imagine their existence now? Could we have imagined only 20 years ago that today we would not be able to survive without smart phones (cell phones are not even good enough anymore), laptops, high-speed internet, email, Facebook, Twitter, Bluetooth, MP3 players, DVD/Blu-ray players, flat-screen HDTVs, satellite TV, and GPS? Can we realistically expect not to care about participating in future technological advances, especially if they are required to communicate with and attract the interest of our grandchildren and great-grandchildren? All of these will require money.

Many people are hoping to increase their standard of living and recreation expenditures in retirement, not cut back. They want to travel more, golf more, and shop more. So why do the "experts" tell us we will only need 70% of our pre-retirement income to enjoy a comfortable retirement?

How can we keep up with the constantly rising cost of everything we will want to buy during retirement if our income never has the opportunity to grow because we are spending all of our investment earnings? We must have a sound income-generation strategy that will allow us to increase our spending over time.

5. Market Declines

Some advisors preach that the only way to overcome inflation is to invest in the stock market. That simply is not true. They quote very long-term average rates of return for the general market, making a point that stocks have outperformed every other asset class for the past 70 years, so it must be the best place to invest now. Of course I am not opposed to investing in the stock market, but we need to take a balanced approach and have realistic expectations for what the outcome might be. Relying too heavily on high expected market returns is a recipe for disappointment and disaster.

As mentioned in Chapter Six, average market returns measured over long periods of time have little application in our personal lives, even though they may be mathematically accurate. Financial decisions have so much more to do with psychology and emotion than with math. Average returns also ignore the question of when we will need to spend money from our investment accounts.

Many people retired in 2007 just before the market crash, with a "solid" plan for how much they thought they could depend on their 401(k) stock and mutual fund investments for income. Then over the course of several months they experienced a huge drop in the value of these investments, some by as much as 50%. Sure, if they stopped taking money out for a few years, their investments might eventually have regained their original value, but what would they do for income in the meantime? Furthermore, after such a scare, how many of them do you think stayed 100% invested so they could have the opportunity to bounce back with the market? Not many.

When one of their investment accounts has just dropped by 50%, most people do not stay invested, even if they understand that they might still be able to earn an average return of 8% over the next 20 years if they keep it in the market. When we see the value of our investments fall, we tend to want to sell out before they drop further and then reinvest only after we have seen the market go back up for a while. Unfortunately, this often results in a much lower rate of return than what the market might have actually produced if we had the discipline to stay invested, as demonstrated by the DALBAR study in Chapter Six.

Have you ever heard the adage, "Buy low and sell high?" It sounds logical, but it is very difficult to implement when we are in the middle of a "great buying opportunity." It does not feel good to buy more investments while watching the value of our current investments drop dramatically. People do not like to hear that they should be happy with an 8% average annual rate of return over a 20-year period even though they might lose 40% one year and gain 50% the next year. That is like telling them they should be happy to put one foot in a bucket of boiling water and the other foot in a bucket of ice water because on average they will be comfortable.

I was discussing this concept with a client of mine who is a surgeon, and he responded, "You're right—that's like telling a patient who has an infection that there was only a 1% chance of him catching it. He doesn't care how small the chances were, because he is in that 1%, and he is suffering 100% of the consequences of acquiring the infection."

While building investments, market declines can actually help us more than they hurt us because they provide opportunities to grow our money more quickly. How can we ever buy low and sell high if the market never drops? When market values fall, we are able to buy more shares of stock than before because each share is "on sale." This phenomenon allows our investments to grow more quickly over time than if the market always remained level, assuming of course that the share prices for the stocks we buy are eventually higher than what we paid for them.

However, when we become dependent on our investments for income, market declines have the opposite effect. When investment values decline, we need to liquidate more shares to maintain a constant income. Then when markets recover, our investments stand less of a chance of regaining their original value because we own fewer shares than we did before. In other words, even if we are emotionally disciplined enough to stay invested when times get tough, we may be forced to liquidate our investments at depressed values just to pay our bills if all of our money is in the market. This may reduce the total balance of our investments much more quickly than if the market was to remain level. It all depends on how the timing of our need for money corresponds with the timing of market cycles.

How big of a difference can this timing make? It can make all the difference in the world. The following diagram shows two different accounts, each invested in the S&P 500 Index. In each example, the investor started with $1,000,000 and took out $80,000 each year for five years. The only difference is which year they started taking the withdrawals.

Year	S&P 500 Total Return	Beg. Year Account Value	Beg. Year Annual Account Distribution	End Year Account Value
1995	38%	$1,000,000	$80,000	$1,265,552
1996	23%	$1,265,552	$80,000	$1,457,043
1997	33%	$1,457,043	$80,000	$1,836,150
1998	29%	$1,836,150	$80,000	$2,258,057
1999	21%	$2,258,057	$80,000	$2,635,667
2000	-9%	$1,000,000	$80,000	$836,188
2001	-12%	$836,188	$80,000	$666,202
2002	-22%	$666,202	$80,000	$456,417
2003	29%	$456,417	$80,000	$484,147
2004	11%	$484,147	$80,000	$448,644

Source: Pinnacle Data Corp

Notice the difference in the "End Year Account Value" at the end of the five-year period for each account. I am amazed that the first investor's account grew to $2,635,667 at the end of five years even though she had taken out $80,000 per year. I am just as amazed that the second investor ended up with only $448,644 even though he had taken only the same $80,000 each year, just because he started five years later.

This demonstrates how much the timing of market performance can impact the long-term viability of reliable income from investment accounts, especially if they are our only source of income during retirement. We never know when the market will drop again, or how much money we will need to take out in the year that it drops. When a large withdrawal corresponds with a large drop in market value, the account can become totally depleted very quickly.

Try telling the investor who took out 8% of $1,000,000 from 2000-2004 that he should still be okay for the rest of his life because over the past 20 years the S&P 500 has averaged 8.2% and over the past 70 years it has averaged 10.4%. What good did the averages do for him? If he had continued taking out $80,000 per year while invested in the S&P 500, he would have been totally out of money by the end of 2010, without even being able to increase his annual income to keep up with inflation. That is not what I call a secure retirement. I want to be sure my clients' retirement income strategy will work no matter when they decide to hang up the hat, regardless of market timing.

As I mentioned earlier, I am not opposed to investing in stocks. I own stocks because I still believe they have a higher potential return than most other asset classes. We just need to be realistic about what rate of return we can expect and how much their value can fluctuate in the short run. We also need to be prudent about the percentage of assets we keep in stocks so we will not be forced to liquidate them during the bad times just to be able to pay our bills.

6. Living Too Long

In the later years of retirement, many people experience a curious psychological transition. Their fear of dying too soon evolves into a fear of living too long. Life can be very challenging during long periods of constant physical pain, mental illness, loneliness, or poverty. No one wants to be a burden on their children or other extended family members. This is why we must be sure to have enough money to provide for ourselves no matter how long we might live.

Has anyone ever shown you when you are going to die? The median life expectancy for a 35-year-old man in good health is approximately 50 years. This means that half of the men in this group will die before age 85 and the other half will die after age

85. However, approximately 85% of these men will live to at least age 70, 63% will live to at least age 80, and 27% will live to at least age 90. Women with similar health tend to live several years longer than men in their same age group.

The bottom line is that although most of us hope for a long and healthy life, we never know how much time we have left. Our lives could be cut short in an instant or strung out much longer than we had anticipated. We must be adequately prepared for either possibility. This reality makes retirement income planning quite challenging. If we knew for sure we only had five more years to live, we could spend more freely in order to really enjoy our last few years together. On the other hand, if we knew our savings had to last another thirty years, we would spend much more conservatively.

Imagine being a coach in an NBA championship game with no game clock, where the referees could end the game at any time with the blow of a whistle. What would your strategy be? Would you run a nonstop full-court press and encourage your players to take lots of quick outside shots in case the game ended after only 30 minutes, or would you take a slower pace so they could endure a game that could potentially last all day? This is how retirement feels to some people.

Although we do not know exactly when we will die, having an idea of how long we are likely to live is still helpful, based on how long most of the people in our situation are living. Have you ever drawn out a timeline that shows where you currently stand on your expected life span? It can be pretty sobering. Here is an example for a 35-year-old who is likely to live to age 85:

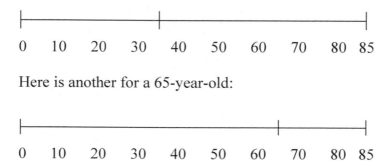

Here is another for a 65-year-old:

Now draw your own. Where do you currently stand on your expected life span? What about your spouse?

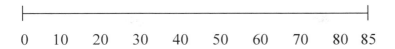

In addition to ensuring that our retirement income strategy is adequate to meet our needs despite inflation and market fluctuations, we need to make sure it will meet our needs regardless of how long we might live. We also need to make sure that we would not be leaving our spouse destitute if we predeceased him or her. My wife is healthier than I am and six years younger, so she will probably outlive me. Therefore, in our personal planning we have put contingencies in place so she will always be okay financially after I am gone, no matter when that might be.

7. Health Care Expenses

A major concern for many retirees today is whether they will be able to afford the rapidly rising cost of health care, especially as their health deteriorates and they become more dependent on the availability of quality care. Medicare is currently the primary provider of health insurance benefits to retirees, but it is in even bigger financial trouble than Social Security. In its official 2011 "Message to the Public," the Social Security and Medicare Board of Trustees stated the following:

> "Both Social Security and Medicare, the two largest federal programs, face substantial cost growth in the upcoming decades due to factors that include population aging as well as the growth in expenditures per beneficiary. Through the mid-2030s, due to the large baby-boom generation entering retirement and lower-birth-rate generations entering employment, population aging is the largest single factor contributing to cost growth in the two programs. Thereafter, the continued rapid growth in health care cost per beneficiary becomes the larger factor...

"Relative to the combined Social Security Trust Funds, the Medicare HI Trust Fund faces a more immediate funding shortfall... Medicare costs are projected to grow substantially from approximately 3.6 percent of GDP in 2010 to 5.5 percent of GDP by 2035... Medicare's HI Trust Fund is expected to pay out more in hospital benefits and other expenditures than it receives in income in all future years. The projected date of HI Trust Fund exhaustion is 2024, five years earlier than estimated in last year's report...

"Projected long-run program costs for both Medicare and Social Security are not sustainable under currently scheduled financing, and will require legislative corrections if disruptive consequences for beneficiaries and taxpayers are to be avoided."[27]

What kind of legislative changes are they alluding to? In order for these programs to continue, eventually there must be a cut in benefits, an increase in taxes, or both. Any of these solutions could have a significant impact on the quality of life retirees will experience in the future.

Another major concern among retirees is the formidable cost of long term care services, which includes nursing home, assisted living, hospice, and home health care expenses. As stated in Chapter Five, the cost of long term care has increased dramatically over the past several years, at a rate much higher than the general inflation rate. According to the U.S. Department of Health and Human Services, "About 70 percent of people over age 65 will require some type of long-term care services during their lifetime. More than 40 percent will need care in a nursing home. On average, someone who is 65 today will need some type of long-term care services and supports for three years."[28] In 2011 the median annual cost nationwide for a private room in a nursing home was $77,745.[29] Medicare does not cover most of these types of expenses.

8. Taxes

It is not how much we make, but how much we get to keep that counts. Are tax rates higher or lower today than they have been historically? Do you think tax rates will go up or down in the future? Will you be in a lower tax bracket when you retire, as conventional wisdom often states?[30]

At the time of this writing (2011), the highest marginal federal income tax rate is 35%. This means that taxable income over $379,150 is taxed at 35%. Do you know what the highest tax rate has been historically? In 1944 and 1945 it was 94% for taxable income over $200,000. Of course far fewer people were making over $200,000 per year back then, but the fact that the tax rate has been as high as 94% for any income level is still staggering. In 1913, when the U.S. federal income tax was first instituted, the top marginal rate was only 7% for taxable income over $500,000. Since then, there have only been 16 years in which the top marginal rate was lower than it is today. For 49 years since 1913, the top rate has been at least 70%.

The chart on the next page outlines the history of the top marginal U.S. federal income tax rate from 1913 to 2010. Look at how unpredictable tax policy can be. Someone making $300,000 in 1941 might have felt pretty good about his tax situation since he would not reach the top bracket of 81% until making over $5,000,000. Can you imagine his horror to learn in 1942 that he would have to pay an 88% tax on any income over $200,000 for the next two years, then 94% for two years after that?

In 1931 the top rate was 25% for income over $100,000, then the very next year it jumped to 63% for income over $1,000,000. In 1986 the top rate was 50% for income over $175,250, and then just two years later it dropped to 28% for income over $29,750. What was the reasoning behind these dramatic changes? Can anyone predict what tax rates will be in the future?

Note	Year	Top Rate	Top Earned Income Rate If Different	On Taxable Income Over	Note	Year	Top Rate	Top Earned Income Rate If Different	On Taxable Income Over
	1913	7.00		500,000	7	1962	91.00		400,000
	1914	7.00		500,000	7	1963	91.00		400,000
	1915	7.00		500,000		1964	77.00		400,000
	1916	15.00		2,000,000		1965	70.00		200,000
	1917	67.00		2,000,000		1966	70.00		200,000
	1918	77.00		1,000,000		1967	70.00		200,000
	1919	73.00		1,000,000		1968	75.25		200,000
	1920	73.00		1,000,000		1969	77.00		200,000
	1921	73.00		1,000,000		1970	71.75		200,000
	1922	58.00		200,000		1971	70.00	60.00	200,000
	1923	43.50		200,000		1972	70.00	50.00	200,000
	1924	46.00		500,000		1973	70.00	50.00	200,000
	1925	25.00		100,000		1974	70.00	50.00	200,000
	1926	25.00		100,000		1975	70.00	50.00	200,000
	1927	25.00		100,000		1976	70.00	50.00	200,000
	1928	25.00		100,000		1977	70.00	50.00	203,200
	1929	24.00		100,000		1978	70.00	50.00	203,200
	1930	25.00		100,000		1979	70.00	50.00	215,400
	1931	25.00		100,000		1980	70.00	50.00	215,400
	1932	63.00		1,000,000		1981	69.13	50.00	215,400
	1933	63.00		1,000,000		1982	50.00		85,600
	1934	63.00		1,000,000		1983	50.00		109,400
	1935	63.00		1,000,000		1984	50.00		162,400
	1936	79.00		5,000,000		1985	50.00		169,020
	1937	79.00		5,000,000		1986	50.00		175,250
	1938	79.00		5,000,000		1987	38.50		90,000
	1939	79.00		5,000,000	8	1988	28.00		29750
	1940	81.10		5,000,000	8	1989	28.00		30950
	1941	81.00		5,000,000	8	1990	28.00		32450
	1942	88.00		200,000		1991	31.00		82,150
	1943	88.00		200,000		1992	31.00		86,500
2	1944	94.00		200,000		1993	39.60		89,150
2	1945	94.00		200,000		1994	39.60		250,000
3	1946	86.45		200,000		1995	39.60		256,500
3	1947	86.45		200,000		1996	39.60		263,750
4	1948	86.45		400,000		1997	39.60		271,050
4	1949	86.45		400,000		1998	39.60		278,450
	1950	84.36		400,000		1999	39.60		283,150
5	1951	91.00		400,000		2000	39.60		288,350
6	1952	92.00		400,000		2001	39.10		297,350
6	1953	92.00		400,000		2002	38.60		307,050
7	1954	91.00		400,000		2003	35.00		311,950
7	1955	91.00		400,000		2004	35.00		319,100
7	1956	91.00		400,000		2005	35.00		326,450
7	1957	91.00		400,000		2006	35.00		336,550
7	1958	91.00		400,000		2007	35.00		357,700
7	1959	91.00		400,000		2008	35.00		357,700
7	1960	91.00		400,000		2009	35.00		372,950
7	1961	91.00		400,000		2010	35.00		

Footnotes

1 This figure is cited when the top marginal rate for earned income differs from that for unearned income.

2 For 1944-1945, the highest tax rate was subject to a maximum effective rate limitation equal to 90% of statutory "net income."

3 For 1946-1947, the highest rate was subject to a maximum effective rate limitation equal to 85.5% of statutory "net income."

4 For 1948-1949, the highest tax rate was subject to a maximum effective rate limitation equal to 77% of statutory "net income."

5 For 1951, the highest tax rate was subject to a maximum effective rate limitation equal to 87.2% of statutory "net income."

6 For 1952-1953, the highest tax rate was subject to a maximum effective rate limitation equal to 88% of statutory "net income."

7 For 1954-1963, the highest tax rate was subject to a maximum effective rate limitation equal to 87% of statutory "taxable income."

8 For 1988-1990, some taxpayers faced a 33% marginal tax rate in an income bracket above the one cited for the 28% rate. However, the marginal rate returned to 28%

Source (through 2003: Truth In Politics

After seeing this chart, how confident do you feel in your ability to forecast what tax rates will be when you retire? When we plan for retirement, we have the tendency to assume constant tax rates. However, tax rates will not remain constant. Therefore, we should be prepared for a wide variety of possible scenarios.

The lowest tax brackets are also very unpredictable. In 2011 the lowest bracket was 10% on the first $17,000 of income for a married couple filing jointly. In the past it has been as low as 0%, but from 1944 to 1963 the lowest bracket ranged from 20% to 23%.[31] Can you imagine the impact a 20% tax would have on low-income families today?

So far we have only discussed ordinary income tax rates, but what about taxes on investment income? Those can change dramatically, too. The current maximum long-term capital gains rate is 15% (for investments held for more than one year). In the past, the maximum capital gains rate has been as high as 39.875% (1976-1978).

The government has kept tax rates relatively low for the past several years in an effort to stimulate the economy by giving consumers more money to spend. How much longer can they keep that going in the face of our country's overwhelming amount of debt, which currently stands at about $15 trillion and continues to grow by over $1 trillion every year?

Have you ever stopped to contemplate how massive $1 trillion really is? Sometimes I think we hear these astronomical figures thrown around so much that we have no concept of how big they really are. If I were to manually count one dollar bill per second, 24 hours a day, it would take me eleven-and-a-half days to count to a million dollars. How long would it take me to count a billion dollar bills? Almost 32 years. How long for a trillion? Almost 32,000 years. This means that it would take me 480,000 years to count out the 15 trillion dollars of debt our country currently owes, counting one dollar per second. That is a lot of money. In the long run, do you think tax rates will go up, down, or remain constant?

What will be the impact on our spendable income in retirement if tax rates are higher than we expected and all of our income is subject to ordinary income tax rates at a time when our deductions are lower than ever because our kids are gone and our mortgage is paid off? It might be a good idea to prepare now for possible tax increases by making sure that not all of our retirement income will be subject to ordinary income taxes.

9. Desire to Leave a Legacy

Often people refrain from spending as much as they would like to spend in retirement because they do not want to leave their spouse destitute when they pass away. They may also plan to leave something to their children, grandchildren, or favorite charity. They may wish to leave a unique legacy by funding the building of a school, a scholarship fund, or a non-profit foundation for a cause they support, thus making a lasting contribution to society rather than just having fun during retirement.

These two objectives do not necessarily have to be in opposition to one another. Why not enjoy a rewarding retirement *and* leave a lasting legacy?

Eliminating Threats to a Secure Retirement

Does this sound overwhelming? For most people, retirement does not turn out to be what they envisioned it would be because they were not adequately equipped to address these issues. Fortunately, with proper preparation we can eliminate all of these threats and enjoy a secure, comfortable retirement regardless of external forces over which we have no control.

1. Save Enough, Invest Wisely, and Get Out of Debt

Some of the solutions to these threats are fairly simple. Simple does not always mean easy, though. The principles we have discussed in this book can help us overcome all of the challenges listed above. If we have the discipline to consistently save at least 20% of our gross income throughout our full-time working years, invest it wisely, and eliminate all debt by the time we plan to slow down, we will have won half the battle.

2. Conquer Inflation, Longevity, and Legacy Concerns

How can we overcome the effects of inflation? The most obvious answer is simply to have more money. I know some people who have accumulated so much money that they have no concerns about inflation. They could face double-digit inflation for the rest of their lives and still not even come close to spending all of their wealth. They have earned the freedom to keep all of their assets in safe, stable investments without really needing much growth over time. They enjoy complete peace of mind and a total disinterest in the financial news.

However, since not everyone is able to accumulate that much money, we need other sound strategies to increase our spendable retirement income over time without incurring the risk of running out of money before we die. Real assets, such as real estate, tend to fare better during inflationary periods than cash instruments, such as bank accounts. If I own rental real estate, the amount of rent I can collect is likely to generally increase over time along with inflation. The market value of my property is also likely to increase during inflationary periods, thus helping my income keep pace with the generally rising cost of everything else I will need to buy throughout retirement. This obviously does not always occur, as we saw in the real estate crash of 2008, but in "normal times" tends to be the case.

Working in some capacity during retirement also can help to overcome the effects of inflation because as the cost of everything else goes up, typically the amount of money we can earn goes up, too. For example, let's say I am 65 years old and have $4,000,000 in an investment account consistently earning 4% tax-free every year. If I were to spend $240,000 from that account in the first year of retirement and increase my income by 3% per year to keep up with inflation, I would be totally out of money by age 83, only 18 years into retirement. If I could somehow bring in just $80,000 a year after tax by working part-time, increase my employment income by 3% per year, and reduce the distributions from my investment account proportionately, my investment account would last all the way to age 93 without reducing my lifestyle.

Delaying retirement is another way to increase the likelihood that our investments will continue to provide stable income for the rest of our lives while keeping up with inflation. Let's say I decide to work full-time until age 70 instead of retiring at age 65, and then continue to work part-time as described in the example above after age 70. This would give me five more years to save for retirement, five more years for my investments to grow, five fewer years of relying on my investments for income, and five fewer years of allowing inflation to take its toll on my spending power. Given all the same facts as in the previous example, but saving an additional $100,000 a year from ages 65-69 and waiting until age 70 to take income from the investments, at age 93 my investment account would still be worth a little over $3,900,000, and I would not run out of money until age 104.

Another strategy for overcoming inflation during retirement is to own a fully funded whole life insurance policy with a guaranteed death benefit. How can that be? Due to their fear of running out of money too soon, many people spend only the interest income their investments are earning so the principal balance will remain intact. For example, if I am 65 years old and own $4,000,000 in investments earning 4% tax-free as in the example above, I might be unable or unwilling to work part-time or delay retirement to make my investments last longer. Instead, I might decide to cut my lifestyle way back and only spend the $160,000 of interest income earned each year. I might not ever feel like I could afford to increase my income to keep up with inflation because I would be afraid to allow my account balance to dip below $4,000,000. I would feel locked out of spending any of the principal because I know that if I spent $240,000 per year without working and increased my withdrawals by 3% per year, then I would be totally out of money by age 83. What if I live to age 90, or what if my spouse lives another 10 years after I am gone?

On the other hand, if in addition to the $4,000,000 investment account I also owned a paid-up whole life insurance policy that is guaranteed to pay my spouse or other heirs $4,000,000 when I die, how much more income could I afford to take from my investments during retirement? Well, if I expected to live until age 83, then there would be no problem with spending

$240,000 and increasing my income by 3% each year to keep up with inflation. If I died "on time" at age 83, my spouse or other heirs would receive the $4,000,000 death benefit from my whole life policy to replenish my original investment account balance, and we would have been able to spend a little more than $5,650,000 total from our investment account together over those 18 years. That is almost twice as much as we could have spent if we had been living only off of the 4% investment earnings for those 18 years. We would have succeeded in overcoming the impact of inflation because we would have been able to spend a lot more money together.

What if I died before age 83? Then my heirs would receive the $4,000,000 death benefit plus whatever investments had not yet been spent. What if I lived past age 83? By this point the cash value in my whole life insurance policy, which is the amount I can spend while I am still alive, would be worth almost as much as the death benefit. This means that for many years to come I could start taking at least as much income from my whole life insurance policy as I had been taking from my other investments, so I will still be okay. Then when I did pass away, the amount I had not yet spent from my whole life policy would be left to my heirs.

Having a guaranteed death benefit in place may allow me to increase my retirement income by using other assets in ways that I may never have considered if I did not own permanent life insurance. For example, the presence of a promised payout to my heirs upon my death might give me the psychological permission to take out a reverse mortgage on my home, which would provide additional guaranteed income for as long as my spouse and I live. Then the life insurance death benefit could be used to pay back the note when I die and leave the house to my heirs unencumbered. I may never choose to do this even with a whole life policy in force, but at least it becomes a more viable option than it would be without the insurance.

Instead of spending the entire principal balance from my investments over an 18-year period, I might decide instead to acquire guaranteed lifetime income from an annuity. This would probably give me a similar amount of annual income as an 18-year payout of principal and interest, but the income would not stop at age 83 as it did in the example above. Much like a pension, I would continue to receive guaranteed income until death, even if I lived to age 120 or longer. The disadvantage with this strategy is that the income to my family would stop if I died earlier than expected. Since the life insurance death benefit would replace the investment values to my heirs, it is the key to making this option a possibility.

We cannot forecast what exactly would be the best combination of strategies to overcome inflation when we retire. We can decide that when we get there, based on current economic conditions, our actual investment mix, and our income needs at the time. The point is that working for as long as possible, even if just part-time, is a great hedge against inflation. In addition, the guaranteed death benefit provided by a whole life insurance policy can empower our other assets to generate much greater retirement income than they could produce otherwise—perhaps even two to three times as much income, without taking any additional risk. These examples also demonstrate that whole life insurance mitigates the risk of living too long, especially when used in conjunction with a life annuity, without leaving our spouse or other heirs destitute. Of course the death benefit must be absolutely guaranteed by a very stable insurance company, or these strategies will not work.

3. Protect against Market Declines

That's enough about inflation, longevity, and legacy solutions. How do we solve the problem of market risk? One strategy for avoiding the negative impact of dramatic market declines on retirement income is to maintain at least a few years' worth of income in more stable asset classes such as CDs, bonds, whole life insurance, and annuities. Since these typically are not affected by market fluctuations, when the market crashes we can take income from these stable assets in order to give our stocks, mutual funds, ETFs, REITs, or other market-driven assets a chance to rebound when the market recovers, without having to suffer a drop in income. Then, after the market rebounds, we can sell off some of our market-based assets to replenish our stable assets in preparation for the next crash, but we would not have been forced to sell any of them at depressed prices.

Pensions, although not as reliable as they used to be, are still a great source of stable retirement income not directly related to personal investment performance. These are harder to come by these days, since most employers have discontinued them, but those of us who are not entitled to a pension can derive similar guaranteed income for life from annuities, as mentioned above. In fact, annuity income from a very stable life insurance company may be even more secure than many of today's employer-provided pensions.

One type of annuity provides a set amount of income for life without any regard to market performance. The main advantage of this type is that it provides the highest guaranteed monthly payout for the rest of the investor's life. However, the investor's income has no potential to increase, and when she dies the income completely stops, with no residual value left for heirs. Variations of this type of annuity allow the investor to exchange a little lower monthly payout for a guaranteed "period certain," such as 10 or 20 years. This means that even if she were to die before the end of the elected period, the insurance company would be required to continue making the same monthly payments to her beneficiaries until the end of the elected period.

Another type of annuity allows the investor to stay in the market while providing guaranteed minimum income for life, which is typically 5-6% of the initial account value per year, regardless of how the market performs. This strategy provides the potential for substantial growth without the risk of losing retirement income. If the market performs well, the investor's income could go up over time, but if it does not perform well, at least the guaranteed minimum income will be paid for as long as the investor and his or her spouse live, even if the account value drops to zero. If any money is left in the account upon the death of both spouses, their beneficiaries would receive it.

How is this possible? Although it may sound too good to be true, we must remember how insurance and annuities work. Insurance companies rely on the law of large numbers, which states that the higher the number of random individuals in a pool, the closer the actual loss experience of the pool will approximate the estimated loss experience. In other words, when companies insure very large numbers of people, their risk may be nearly eliminated because they can very accurately predict the amount they will have to pay out to beneficiaries. They can rely on average rates of return and average life expectancy rates when they own a statistically significant pool of those who form the averages. Of course they cannot always perfectly predict loss experience, which is why they are required to maintain very large reserves, but they usually estimate losses remarkably well.

On the other hand, as individual investors we cannot personally rely on average rates of return or average life expectancy rates because our personal outcome may be very different from the average outcome. For example, although the average rate of return in the stock market might be 8% over the next 20 years, my personal rate of return might only end up being 3%. Likewise, although average life expectancy for a 65-year-old man might be age 85, he has no guarantee of dying at age 85. He might only live to age 66, or he might live to age 100.

If my personal experience ended up being very different from the average, then the consequences could be devastating to my family and me without the guarantees that life insurance and annuities provide. However, the consequences of my unexpected loss would be almost unnoticeable to a very large, stable insurance company because they would be covering so many other people whose experience as a whole would very closely approximate the average.

Although we cannot personally "own the average," insurance companies can if they insure enough people. We essentially purchase partial ownership of the average by paying a fee to an insurance company. In other words, insurance and annuities allow us to vicariously benefit from the certainty that the average experience of a pool of millions of other people provides. Insurance companies can fairly compensate those in the pool who die too soon or live too long, but we must be active participants in the pool to receive these potential benefits. Due to this fact, when properly employed in tandem, whole life insurance and annuities can be very powerful tools to provide financial security throughout our lives without leaving our loved ones impoverished when we pass away.

4. Cover Health Care and Long Term Care Expenses

Employing the strategies we have discussed to generate more spendable income in retirement will help us meet rising health-care expenses. The future of Medicare is uncertain, but in the meantime, Medicare supplement plans are great for covering the gaps that Medicare will not cover. Long term care insurance plans are also critical as an asset protection strategy. If we ever need long term care services, long term care insurance helps us avoid the risk of depleting our assets to receive quality care.

5. Minimize Taxes

What about taxes? Under current tax law, various types of assets are taxed differently. We should pay close attention now to how our assets may be taxed when we will start taking income from them so we can be in a position to control our tax bracket in retirement. It is not how much we have saved, but how much of it we can spend after taxes that counts.

Traditional retirement savings accounts such as 401(k)s, IRAs, 403(b)s, 457 plans, and pension plans are great places to accumulate money because contributions are tax-deductible and growth is tax-deferred, which means that we do not have to pay taxes on any of the growth until we pull money out of the account. However, these types of accounts are miserable places to take money from because every penny we take out is taxed as ordinary income, not to mention the severe additional penalties for taking money out too soon or leaving it in too long. Thus, people who have all of their savings in these types of accounts will likely be frustrated in retirement because they will be paying the highest possible amount of taxes for the income they take from them.

Stocks, bonds, mutual funds, real estate, privately held businesses, and many other types of investments not held in retirement accounts enjoy long-term capital gains treatment if held for more than one year before sold. This means that any gain in the value of these types of investments tends to be taxed at a lower rate than ordinary income tax when sold, although income from these types of investments may still be subject to

ordinary income tax as it is earned. Distributions from Roth
IRAs, municipal bonds, and whole life insurance may be tax-
free, if properly taken.[32]

Each of these three types of tax treatment has its own advantages and disadvantages. The key is to find balance by owning
some assets in each category. Those who are prepared with
plenty of each type may be able to significantly reduce taxes on
retirement income by taking some income from each category,
based on prevailing tax rates and brackets at the time of distribution.

For instance, under current tax law (2011) a married couple
filing jointly would pay a 10% tax on the first $17,000 of taxable
income, 15% on taxable income between $17,000 and $69,000,
25% between $69,000 and $139,350, 28% from $139,350 to
$212,300, 33% from $212,300 to $379,150, and 35% on all tax-
able income over $379,150. If a retired couple were to take
$240,000 total income for the year from their investments, they
may not wish to subject all of it to ordinary income tax rates.

In order to reduce their tax bill they might choose to take only $69,000 from their 401(k)s or IRAs, which would be taxed at
10% and 15% ordinary income rates, $100,000 from non-
qualified stocks or mutual funds taxed at 15% long-term capital
gains rates, and the remaining $71,000 from Roth IRAs, munici-
pal bonds, or whole life insurance tax-free. In this example,
assuming no deductions, and assuming no basis in the non-
qualified stocks or mutual funds, their total tax bill would be
$24,500, a 10.2% effective tax rate.

Conversely, if they had taken the full $240,000 income from
their 401(k)s or IRAs, they would have paid more than twice as
much in taxes: $56,730 total, a 24.6% effective tax rate. If they
had parked all of their available savings in 401(k)s, IRAs, or
pension plans when they were younger, they would have no
choice but to pay the higher taxes or live on a much smaller income in retirement.

As we discussed earlier, taxes have been much higher in the
past than they are today. What if tax rates went back to former
levels? Then the impact would be even more dramatic, and they
probably would wish they owned more assets in tax-free or non-
qualified investments.

We should do whatever we can now to diversify the tax treatment of our assets so we can have the flexibility to manage our tax bracket in retirement. This is not something that can be fixed overnight.

6. Maintain Balance and Seek Professional Advice

Finding proper balance among these recommendations can be a daunting task, but it is critical to retirement success. You must fully understand the benefits and limitations of each potential solution to be sure your strategy will meet your objectives. Thus, I cannot emphasize strongly enough the importance of discussing your specific situation with a competent financial advisor before proceeding with any of these recommendations.

This is not an exhaustive list of options. My intent is to demonstrate that with proper preparation, you can successfully overcome all of these obstacles and enjoy a very secure, comfortable retirement, whether or not you decide to continue working.

10

Leave a Meaningful Legacy

You Can't Take It with You

While recently viewing an exhibit of artifacts from King Tut's tomb, I was reminded of the old adage, "You can't take it with you." I must admit it was hard to imagine how King Tut could really believe that surrounding his dead body with all those ornate objects would do him any good in the next life. The exhibit served as a stark reminder to me that no matter how wealthy or powerful we may be, we all must leave our material possessions behind when we die.

In the words of King Solomon, "As he came forth of his mother's womb, naked shall he return to go as he came, and shall take nothing of his labour, which he may carry away in his hand...and what profit hath he that hath laboured for the wind" (Ecclesiastes 5:15-16). We are only stewards over our belongings for a short time, and then when we die they must be passed on for someone else to enjoy or discard. If our sole objective throughout life was to accumulate wealth, we will be very poor indeed when we die.

Since we know that we must give away everything we own when we die, why not give much of it away while we are still alive and can witness the joy our gifts may grant others? Many wealthy people give major portions of their money away during their lifetime. Doing so often brings them great satisfaction because they can see the difference their money makes in the lives of others.

Financial gifts might be much more meaningful to prospective heirs now than when we die because they may help meet time-sensitive needs that typically arise earlier in life, such as education expenses, business start-up costs, or the down payment on a first home. Our favorite charitable organizations may also benefit more now from what we can give while we are alive than what we intend to give when we die. Furthermore, in turn we may receive a significant current tax deduction for doing so.[33]

Another benefit to giving away smaller portions over time is that we can see how wisely prospective heirs might use money they are scheduled to inherit in much larger quantities later on. Giving while we are alive may also help to significantly reduce estate taxes when we pass away. These types of gifts should be made prudently with the advice of a qualified estate planning or tax attorney so as to maximize the potential tax benefits.

Although we cannot take any material possessions with us when we die, we *can* take many other things with us, such as our relationships with other people, knowledge gained, skills honed, and talents developed. We also will have a full recollection of all our good deeds, as well as ill deeds that were not corrected. We will perfectly recall the extent to which we used our wealth to benefit other people.

No matter how much we gave throughout our lives, I believe that in the end we will all wish we had been even more generous to others. This perspective sparks a less selfish motive for building wealth. Rather than viewing our possessions as status symbols or objects to hoard, we come to view them as tools to help relieve suffering, build relationships, acquire knowledge, and develop talents in order to more effectively serve other people.

Don't Just Leave Money

What are you planning to leave behind? For what do you most want to be remembered? Yes, of course we must all leave behind everything we own. However, our legacy can be much greater and more significant than that. It is somewhat ironic that the most valuable things we can leave for our heirs when we die also happen to be the only things we can take with us, such as our knowledge, faith, love, friendship, and example of good deeds.

Many wealthy people are very concerned about what to do with their wealth when they pass on. They are worried that if they leave too much to their children or grandchildren, it will ruin them. Warren Buffet is giving the vast majority of his wealth, about $36 billion worth, to charity while he is still alive. He explained, "I want to give my kids enough so they could feel that they could do anything, but not so much that they could do nothing."

If children have not learned to love working or do not know how to use money responsibly, an inheritance may be more of a burden to them than a blessing. A properly drafted and funded trust can help to control how they are allowed to use the money, but a risk still certainly exists that too large of an inheritance could rob them of their ambition, industry, humility, and sense of responsibility. However, if we can be certain they will use it wisely, they may be able to do much good with it. It is our responsibility to teach them.

When we come to understand and live by the timeless principles of financial security, we should share them with our family members so they can enjoy financial security throughout their lives and be a greater benefit to society. No amount of money we leave our children could possibly be more valuable than teaching them these principles. Even if I were to leave my children $10 million each, they could spend it all within a year if they were not properly taught. The famous Chinese Proverb comes to mind, "Give a man a fish and you feed him for a day. Teach a man to fish and you feed him for a lifetime."

If we have truly learned to love and serve our fellow man, we will not be content to merely teach our own family members, but will also be anxious to share our knowledge with everyone around us who is willing to listen. When we teach others, we also benefit in turn. I have found that teaching these principles helps me to understand them more fully and reinforces my own efforts to live by them so I can be a good example to those I teach.

When we share with people around us the reasoning behind our desire to improve our financial habits, they can support us and hold us accountable. Surrounding ourselves with people who are striving to live by sound financial principles can help us feel less pressure to spend money on meaningless things we cannot afford, just like hanging out with people who eat healthily and exercise regularly can help us lose weight. They will not ridicule frugality, but will applaud our wise decisions and serve as good examples to us. If our current friends and family do not practice wise financial management, we can educate them so they will no longer undermine our efforts. If we learn to live these principles and teach many others to do so, we may leave a great legacy of financial security for many generations.

Clean Up After Yourself

On a different note, if we are not careful, another thing we may unintentionally leave behind is a disaster that our loved ones will have to clean up. I know several people whose parents, spouse, or other relatives left quite a mess. This is no fun for anyone to sort out, even if the estate is worth a significant amount. Taking the time and effort to organize our finances and communicate openly with our heirs is an important way to demonstrate our love for them.

One such woman who was left to clean up a mess was named as successor trustee and beneficiary of a deceased relative's outdated trust. Her relative manually revised his trust document several times without the assistance of an attorney, so some of the trust language was contradictory when he passed away. Originally he had named a charity as the sole beneficiary of his assets, but later changed the beneficiary to her. Now his estate must be settled in court because the trust does not clearly specify who is legally entitled to his inheritance.

If that were all she had to deal with, it would be a cinch. However, this relative left behind a house filled with belongings very far away from where she lives. She had to sort through, valuate, throw away, and auction off everything herself. As she sorted through files, she found many stock certificates for several old companies which had long since been bought out by other companies. It was quite a process to determine the current company names and values of these shares, and then to convert them into electronic shares in the name of the trust. She also had to deal with the headache of selling his home from out of state.

This whole process has taken years because she could not neglect her own tremendous responsibilities at home, such as running a business, remodeling her home, helping her children, and taking care of a terminally ill family member who was living with her. So far she has not taken compensation from the trust for any of this work because she does not want to be accused of self-dealing. After all of this, the courts may still decide that all of her relative's money should go to charity because of the ambiguity in the trust documents.

She tried several times to get him to sort through everything, have an attorney review his trust, and get better prepared before he passed away, but he simply did not want to deal with it. It would have been so much easier for him to figure everything out than it has been for her. He was trying to leave her a legacy of love, but it has turned out to be a huge nightmare.

The potential consequences of disorganization, lack of communication, and poor preparation are also demonstrated by a young man who passed away very suddenly and unexpectedly, leaving his wife with young children still at home. He had always been the sole breadwinner and handled all of the finances. His wife had no idea what they had or where their financial documents were, so it was very difficult for her to figure things out when he died.

As I helped her sort through it all, it was sad to see how frustrated she was with him for not being better prepared and for not communicating with her about their finances. He did not have many assets, but luckily owned a decent-sized term life insurance policy that he had almost cancelled a few weeks before. It was a term policy that had just reached the end of the ten-year level premium period, so the new annual payment due was about five times higher than before. He told his wife he was not willing to pay that much for it. She encouraged him to at least keep it until he could qualify for another policy, but he never got around to paying the premium.

When he passed away she could not find his policy anywhere or even remember the name of the insurance company. About a week later she received a notice from them warning that the policy would be cancelled if the premium were not paid immediately. With trembling hands, she mailed them a check right away. Fortunately the insurance company received the premium within the 30-day grace period, so they paid her the death benefit in full. If he had passed away just a few weeks later, the story would have been even more tragic.

The first thing I always do with new clients is help them organize all of their personal finances so both spouses know what they have and where everything is. This helps them make better financial decisions going forward because they know exactly where they stand. Being organized also makes the transition much easier for a surviving spouse or surviving children when a family member dies.

We should communicate clearly and regularly with the people who will be most impacted financially by our death or incapacity, even if we do not expect it to happen for a very long time. We do not necessarily have to tell our heirs exactly how much money they will inherit, but they should have some idea of who will be getting what, what they should do with it, who will be administering the estate, which advisors to contact, and where to find wills, trust documents, financial statements, insurance policies, and other important documents.

Legal Documents Worth Their Weight in Gold

Who do we want to receive our possessions when we die, and what do we want them to do with them? How can our heirs avoid estate taxes and probate expenses when we pass away? Who would we want to take care of our minor or handicapped children if we can no longer take care of them due to a premature death or extended coma? Who can we trust to manage our financial affairs or to make sound health care decisions for us if we become mentally incapacitated? How can we officially make these wishes known to our family and to the courts, to be sure that they will be carried out when we are no longer around to verbally communicate them?

We must visit with a qualified attorney who specializes in estate planning to discuss these issues and to determine which legal documents will ensure things will go as we would like after we are gone. Typically these documents include wills, trusts, powers of attorney, health care directives, living wills, and for business owners, buy-sell agreements. An estate planning attorney can also help with asset protection, estate tax avoidance, and gifting strategies.

Once we have these important legal documents in place, we should let our heirs know where to find them and properly title our assets and insurance policies to match the instructions documented. Otherwise, they will be worthless.

For example, trusts are valuable tools because they control who receives our property and what they can do with it after we are gone. However, if our assets are not titled in the name of our trust, they may have to go through probate, which means that a judge will determine who gets what, regardless of what the trust says. Probate is a very expensive, drawn-out, public process that easily can be avoided by properly titling our assets while we are alive.

Property that is jointly owned by two or more people automatically passes to the surviving owner(s) without going through probate. Common examples are bank accounts or homes jointly owned by a married couple. Another example of property that would not go through probate is that which passes automatically to a surviving beneficiary, such as a 401(k), IRA, annuity, or life insurance policy. However, we still may wish to list the trust as owner or beneficiary of these types of assets to reduce potential estate taxes and to control how surviving heirs will use the money.

Without proper planning, estate taxes can have a huge impact on what our heirs end up receiving. In 2011 the top estate tax rate is 35%, but a single decedent may pass up to $5,000,000 of assets and life insurance death benefits to heirs estate-tax-free. In other words, estate taxes would only be assessed on property or insurance valued in excess of $5,000,000. Unless the law is changed, in 2013 the top estate tax rate is scheduled to revert to 55% and the exemption amount will be reduced to $1,000,000. This means that if a single woman with a $2,000,000 estate died in 2013, her heirs would have to pay an estate tax of $550,000 within nine months of her passing.

This significant tax often causes quite a dilemma for heirs, especially if most of the value of the estate is found in illiquid assets such as real estate or small business holdings. How can they come up with such a large sum of money to pay the taxes due so quickly without having to sell property at a steep discount? Life insurance is a great tool for delivering a large sum of cash just at the right moment so assets that are important for the family to keep or are very difficult to sell quickly at a reasonable price will not have to be liquidated right away to cover the estate taxes due.

An unlimited amount of assets and life insurance can be passed without any estate tax to a spouse who is a U.S. citizen, but then estate taxes may be due when the spouse passes away. Estate taxes can be significantly reduced or completely avoided through properly drafted trust documents and properly titled assets and insurance.

Many people who understand the importance of drafting estate planning documents delay doing so because they cannot decide who should receive their property or who should take care of their kids. Sometimes spouses disagree so strongly on this topic that they do nothing. As hard as it may be to decide these matters, keep in mind that if we fail to put our decisions in writing before we pass, the courts will decide for us after we are gone, and much of our estate may be lost to probate expenses and estate taxes. How much more likely are they to appoint the guardians we would choose for minor children or to distribute our assets in a manner with which we would be pleased?

Also remember that a disorganized estate often results in fighting among heirs and thousands of dollars wasted on legal fees. How tragic it is that many families become so embittered toward one another after the settlement of an estate that they may never even speak to each other again! I would rather have all of my money go to charity than to have my kids and grandkids fight over it.

I am puzzled by people who work very hard and sacrifice much throughout their lives to accumulate a great fortune, yet show little interest in planning the disposition of their assets when they die. It seems like such a waste for large portions of carefully managed estates to be confiscated by the government, which often is the case for multi-millionaires without proper estate planning.

For example, less than $3 million of Elvis Presley's $10 million estate was left to his heirs after estate taxes and other fees that could have been avoided through proper planning. Howard Hughes mentioned several times that he wanted his $2.5 billion estate to go towards medical research, but he never put it in writing, so his intended gift was never carried out and the estate had to pay hundreds of millions of dollars in estate taxes that might have been avoided. He died without even a will, so his estate was eventually split among twenty-two of his cousins by the courts many years after his death.

I wonder how many deceased multi-millionaires are rolling in their graves because their heirs have squandered overnight what they worked very hard to accumulate over a lifetime. This situation can easily be avoided by spending only a few hours and a few thousand dollars to put instructions in place that would protect spendthrift heirs from themselves and preserve a more meaningful legacy.

Once in place, we should review our estate planning documents periodically to ensure that they still reflect our current wishes, especially after moving to a new state, getting divorced, getting re-married, or adding a new child to the family. We should also periodically review the titles and beneficiary designations of all property and insurance we own.

I know of women who divorced their husbands but never changed the beneficiary designations on their life insurance policies or 401(k)s. When they passed away, their ex-husbands automatically received these assets, and no one could contest it. I have also heard of children who were left out of an inheritance because they were never added to the family trust after they were born. A common problem in the case of blended families is that if the husband dies first with no trust in place, his new wife will likely inherit all of his assets, and then when she passes away, her children will probably inherit them, even if he intended for his children to eventually inherit his assets. All of these unintended consequences can easily be avoided through properly written and regularly updated legal documents, titling of assets, and beneficiary designations.

Consult with a qualified estate planning attorney as soon as possible to discuss these issues and have the necessary documents properly drafted or updated. Do not try to do this on your own, even if you are an attorney who does not specialize in estate planning. I have seen too many improperly drafted documents, even by attorneys. It is not good enough to simply have a will or a trust. Meeting with a qualified attorney to be sure the job is done right is well worth the time and money. These issues are too important to take any chances on getting it wrong.

Be Mindful of Your Legacy

If we are mindful of the legacy we leave behind, we can be of great benefit to our children, grandchildren, and society, not only throughout our lives, but also after we die. Think of the inheritance you have received from your parents, grandparents, teachers, and others who have greatly enhanced your life. For what are you most grateful to them? Do you most value their financial gifts, or the lessons they taught and the love they gave? Strive to give just as much or even more to your posterity, in the most meaningful ways possible.

Also think of the rich inheritance we have all received from the multitude of forefathers who have greatly impacted our lives, even though we have never met them. We may never fully appreciate the legacy of the founding fathers, other great statesmen, and soldiers of this country, who have given their lives for the freedoms we now enjoy. We may never fully realize the legacy of countless scientists, inventors, and entrepreneurs who have worked tirelessly and sacrificed much to collectively create the wonderful standard of living we now enjoy. We may never have the opportunity to adequately thank the many spiritual leaders, authors, composers, and artists who uplift us and help us find meaning in life. We must demonstrate our gratitude to these benefactors by continuing to improve the greatness of our society through the legacy we leave behind.

11

Decide Your Next Step

Knowledge Alone is Not Power

In his landmark book entitled *Think and Grow Rich,* Napoleon Hill taught, "Knowledge will not attract money, unless it is organized and directed through practical plans for the specific purpose of accumulating money. Lack of understanding of this fact has been the source of confusion to millions of people who falsely believe that 'knowledge is power.' It is nothing of the sort! Knowledge is only *potential* power. It becomes power only when, and if, it is organized into definite plans of action and directed to a definite end."[34]

Throughout this book we have discussed timeless principles of financial security which, if strictly followed, will help us enjoy prosperity and maintain dignity and freedom throughout our entire lives, despite any unexpected events which may threaten to financially devastate us. Learning the principles is easy, but they do not do us any good unless we consistently apply them. Unfortunately, that is the hard part.

Regardless of where you live, I would be happy to help you determine how to properly apply these principles to your personal situation or answer any additional questions you may have. Just send me an email at adam_dawson@wealthsg.com.

As you strive to incorporate what you have learned in this book, be patient with yourself and start with realistic goals. Remember that obtaining financial security is more like running a marathon, not a 50-yard dash. It cannot be accomplished overnight. Focus on your most critical shortfalls first, and then gradually move toward the next step. For example, if you lack adequate insurance or liquid savings, get that squared away before paying off debts or contributing to retirement plans. Always maintain financial balance along the way.

Summary of Principles

Here is a general summary of the most critical principles of financial security we have discussed, in order of priority:

1. Be honest in all financial dealings with others, whether they are individuals or large institutions. Pay all obligations fully and on time.
2. Donate at least 10% of gross income to tithing or other charitable causes.
3. Fully protect assets and income through proper types and amounts of insurance.
4. Save at least 20% of gross income for the future before spending any of it.
5. Maintain at least three months' worth of liquid cash and food storage.
6. Ensure complementary balance among various investment objectives and methods of tax treatment.
7. Minimize investment risk, invest primarily in what you understand, and be content with modest gains. Avoid high-risk investments and get-rich-quick schemes.
8. Avoid and eliminate debt. Forget about the Joneses. Incur manageable, low-interest debts only when necessary for a modest home, basic vehicle, or education that is likely to improve income. Pay cash for everything else.
9. Work as long as your health permits, even if just part-time, and learn to love it. Continually improve earning power and flexibility through additional education.
10. Leave a meaningful legacy. Organize and protect your estate with valid legal documents and properly titled assets. Teach as many people as possible what you have learned.

Where Do You Stand?

How well do you currently apply each of these major principles in your life? Rating yourself here will help you determine what should be your next step to attain greater financial security for yourself and for your family:

1. Are you honest in all financial dealings, and do you pay your obligations fully and on time?
   a. Seldom
   b. Often
   c. Always
2. Percentage of gross income currently going to charity:
   a. 0-4%
   b. 5-9%
   c. 10%+
3. Current level of protection for assets and income:
   a. Very little or no insurance
   b. Some of the types and amounts of insurance recommended in Chapter Five
   c. All of the recommended types and amounts
4. Percentage of gross income regularly going to savings or investments:
   a. 0-9%
   b. 10-19%
   c. 20%+
5. Current amount of liquid cash and food storage:
   a. Less than one month's worth of living expenses and amount of food normally eaten
   b. One to two months
   c. Three months or more
6. How well-balanced are you among various investment objectives and methods of tax treatment?
   a. All savings and investments in one type
   b. At least a little in a few different types, but highly concentrated in one type
   c. Well-balanced among several complementary types

7. How much risk do you take with the majority of your in-
    vestments?
    a. I frequently risk everything in hopes of big short-
        term gains
    b. Sometimes I take big risks with a large portion of
        my investable assets
    c. I always seek to minimize risk and if I participate
        in high-risk investments, I only do so only with a
        small percentage of my total investable assets
8. How well do you manage debt?
    a. I carry high-interest or overwhelming amounts of
        debt
    b. I only carry manageable amounts of low-interest
        debt
    c. I am completely debt-free
9. What is your attitude towards work?
    a. I hate working and only do the minimum amount
        required to get by
    b. I work hard to attain my goals, but do not really
        enjoy it
    c. I work very hard to attain my goals and love it
10. How well-organized is your estate?
    a. I have no idea what I would want to happen to my
        property or my kids when I pass away
    b. I know what I would want to happen to my prop-
        erty and my kids when I pass away, but have not
        created valid legal documents to put my wishes in
        writing, or if I have, they have not been reviewed
        for a long time
    c. I have created up-to-date valid legal documents
        that accurately portray my current wishes and
        have titled my assets accordingly

Obviously this questionnaire is over-simplified, but should
give you some idea where you stand and which areas need the
most improvement. Remember that these questions are generally
listed in order of priority, so deficiencies among the first few
questions are more urgent to address than questions at the end of
the list. In case you couldn't tell, "A's" are the worst and "C's"

are the best. If you scored all "C's" then congratulations—you are on the right track! If not, list below some specific goals for improvement. Also specify when you will accomplish them:

Your Action Plan

Specific Goal   Date to be
                                                        Completed

1. _____   _____

2. _____   _____

3. _____   _____

4. _____   _____

5. _____   _____

6. _____   _____

7. _____   _____

8. _____   _____

9. _____   _____

10. _____   _____

Again, be patient with yourself and with others as you strive to live by these principles. Although you may not be able to always follow every principle perfectly, you can at least be perfect in the most critical areas. Do not give up on all of them if there are some that you can never quite master. Every effort you exert to adopt any of them will bring you closer to attaining the lasting financial security you seek.

Remember that the more you share these principles with others, the more your understanding of them and ability to live by them will increase. Everyone wants financial security, peace, and prosperity, but most people struggle to find a clear path they can rely on to attain it. You may save someone's life by showing them the way.

The future is always filled with great hope. If you ever become discouraged, look to the examples of countless people who have enjoyed great freedom and success throughout their lives due to their diligent application of the timeless principles of financial security. You can also enjoy lasting financial security, peace, and prosperity throughout your life if you want it badly enough. You are not just a victim of circumstance.

The choice is yours. Which road will you take?

About the Author

Adam Dawson, CFP® has been building strong and lasting relationships with clients all over the country by providing personalized attention and sound financial guidance since 2000. He holds the distinguished CERTIFIED FINANCIAL PLANNER™ certification in addition to the Series 7, Series 66, and life, disability, and long term care insurance licenses.

Adam graduated from Brigham Young University with a Bachelors Degree in Music Composition and continues to compose, perform, and conduct as his schedule permits. He loves spending as much time as possible with his beautiful wife Andrea and four children. He also enjoys playing basketball, hiking, and camping.

Contact Info:

Adam Dawson, CFP®
8379 West Sunset Road, Suite 140
Las Vegas, NV 89113

Phone: (702) 735-4355
Email: adam_dawson@wealthsg.com

 CERTIFIED FINANCIAL PLANNER™ **CFP**®

Outline of Topics

Index of Quotes

Ecclesiastes 5:12   111

"The sleep of a labouring man is sweet, whether he eat little or much: but the abundance of the rich will not suffer him to sleep."

Ecclesiastes 5:15-16   147

"As he came forth of his mother's womb, naked shall he return to go as he came, and shall take nothing of his labour, which he may carry away in his hand...and what profit hath he that hath laboured for the wind?"

Franklin, Benjamin   19

"Money never made a man happy yet, nor will it. There is nothing in its nature to produce happiness. The more a man has, the more he wants. Instead of its filling a vacuum, it makes one."

Franklin, Benjamin   28

"The eyes of other people are the eyes that ruin us. If all but myself were blind, I should want neither fine clothes, fine houses, nor fine furniture."

Frost, Robert   9

*"Two roads diverged in a yellow wood,
And sorry I could not travel both...
I took the one less traveled by,
And that has made all the difference."*

Genesis 3:17-19   112

"Cursed is the ground for thy sake; in sorrow shalt thou eat of it all the days of thy life; thorns also and thistles shall it bring forth to thee...In the sweat of thy face shalt thou eat bread, till thou return unto the ground..."

Genesis 41   72

Joseph interprets Pharaoh's dream and counsels him to save a fifth part of all the grain produced during the seven years of plenty to prepare for the seven years of famine.

Hill, Napoleon   157

"Knowledge will not attract money, unless it is organized and directed through practical plans for the specific purpose of accumulating money. Lack of understanding of this fact has been the source of confusion to millions of people who falsely believe that 'knowledge is power.' It is nothing of the sort! Knowledge is only potential power. It becomes power only when, and if, it is organized into definite plans of action and directed to a definite end."

Endnotes

[1] Suzanne Austin Alchon, *A Pest in the Land: New World Epidemics in a Global Perspective* (University of New Mexico Press, 2003), 21.

[2] Kim Kenney, "Cars in the 1920s," *American History @Suite 101*, 15 January 2009, <http://kim-kenney.suite101.com/cars-in-the-1920s-a90169> (2 May 2012).

[3] Steven Smith, "Culture of Debt Driven by GM," *Marketplace: The Borrowers*, 9 March 2009, <http://www.marketplace.org/topics/business/borrowers/culture-debt-driven-gm> (2 May 2012).

[4] "The History of FHA," U.S. Department of Housing and Urban Development: The Federal Housing Administration (FHA), <http://portal.hud.gov/hudportal/HUD?src=/program_offices/housing/fhahistory> (3 May 2012).

[5] Ben Woolsey and Emily Starbuck Gerson, "The History of Credit Cards," <http://www.creditcards.com/credit-card-news/credit-cards-history-1264.php> (2 May 2012).

[6] J. Reuben Clark, Jr., *Conference Report* (April 1938), 103.

[7] Laura Ingalls Wilder, *Little House on the Prairie* (New York: HarperCollins Publishers, 1963), 124-125.

[8] CDA Personal Disability Quotient (PDQ) calculator, <http://www.disabilitycanhappen.org/chances_disability/pdq.asp> (21 March 2012).

[9] Council for Disability Awareness, Long-Term Disability Claims Review, 2011, <http://www.disabilitycanhappen.org/research/CDA_LTD_Claims_Survey_2011.asp> (21 March 2012).

[10] "Will You Need LTC?" National Clearinghouse for Long Term Care Information, U.S. Department of Health and Human Services, <http://www.longtermcare.gov/LTC/Main_Site/Understanding/Definition/Know.aspx> (21 March 2012).

[11] "Emerging Trends and Findings," Executive Summary, Genworth 2011 Cost of Care Survey, <http://www.genworth.com/content/etc/medialib/genworth_v2/pdf/ltc_cost_of_care.Par.85518.File.dat/Executive%20Summary_gnw.pdf> (21 March 2012).

[12] "Medicaid Eligibility Requirements," National Clearinghouse for Long Term Care Information, U.S. Department of Health and Human Services, <http://www.longtermcare.gov/LTC/Main_Site/Paying/Public_Programs/Medicaid/Eligibility.aspx#General> (21 March 2012).

[13] Depending on the payment of dividends. Dividends are not guaranteed, but are highly likely to be paid.

[14] We do not provide tax or legal advice. Please consult the appropriate advisor for more information regarding your specific situation.

[15] There is an additional premium cost when the Waiver of Premium Rider is selected on a policy.

[16] "The San Francisco/Oakland Bay Bridge," CA Department of Transportation, <http://www.dot.ca.gov/hq/esc/tollbridge/SFOBB/Sfobbfacts.html> (23 March 2012).

[17] "Personal Saving Rate," U.S. Department of Commerce: Bureau of Economic Analysis, <http://research.stlouisfed.org/fred2/data/PSAVERT.txt> (23 March 2012).

[18] We do not provide tax or legal advice. Please consult the appropriate advisor for more information regarding your specific situation. Policy benefits are reduced by a loan, loan interest and/or withdrawals. Dividends, if any, are affected by policy loans and loan interest. Withdrawals above what is paid into the policy may cause ordinary income taxes to be paid on the gain portion of the policy. If the policy lapses, any withdrawals or loans considered gain in the policy may be subject to ordinary income taxes. If the policy is a Modified Endowment Contract (MEC), there are no loans and any distribution is considered a withdrawal. These withdrawals are distributed as gain first and subject to ordinary income taxes. If the insured is under 59 1/2 the gain portion of the withdrawal is subject to a 10% tax penalty.

[19] The continued contributions by the insurance company in the case of disability are contingent on a separate rider.

[20] Campbell R. Harvey, "Historical Behavior of Asset Returns," *WWWFinanace*, <http://www.duke.edu/~charvey/Classes/ba350/history/history.htm> (30 November 2011).

[21] "Quantitative Analysis of Investor Behavior, 2010," DALBAR, Inc., <www.dalbar.com>. Additional disclosures required by DALBAR:

Equity benchmark performance and systematic equity investing examples are represented by the Standard & Poor's 500 Composite Index, an unmanaged index of 500 common stocks generally considered representative of the U.S. stock market. Indexes do not take into account the fees and expenses associated with investing, and individuals cannot invest directly in any index. Past performance cannot guarantee future results.

Bond benchmark performance and systematic bond investing examples are represented by the Barclays Aggregate Bond Index, an unmanaged index of bonds generally considered representative of the bond market. Indexes do not take into account the fees and expenses associated with investing, and individuals cannot invest directly in any index. Past performance cannot guarantee future results.

Average stock investor, average bond investor and average asset allocation investor performance results are based on a DALBAR study, "Quantitative Analysis of Investor Behavior (QAIB), 2010." DALBAR is an independent, Boston-based financial research firm. Using monthly fund data supplied by the Investment Company Institute, QAIB calculates investor returns as the change in assets after excluding sales, redemptions and exchanges. This method of calculation captures realized and unrealized capital gains, dividends, interest, trading costs, sales charges, fees, expenses and any other costs. After calculating investor returns in dollar terms, two percentages are calculated for the period examined: Total investor return rate and annualized investor return rate. Total return rate is determined by calculating the investor return dollars as a percentage of the net of the sales, redemptions, and exchanges for the period.

Systematic investing examples are hypothetical and for illustrative purposes only. Systematic investing involves continuous investments regardless of security price levels. It cannot assure a profit or protect against a loss in declining markets.

[22] Martin Bashir and Sara Holmberg, "Powerball Winner Says He's Cursed," *ABC 20/20*, 6 April 2007, <http://abcnews.go.com/2020/powerball-winner-cursed/story?id=3012631> (23 March 2012).

[23] Jonah Lehrer, "Don't! The Secret of Self-Control," *The New Yorker*, 18 May 2009.

[24] Richard Nelson Bolles, *What Color Is Your Parachute?* (New York: Ten Speed Press, 1999).

[25] Mark Victor Hansen and Art Linkletter, *How to Make the Rest of Your Life the Best of Your Life* (Nashville: Thomas Nelson, Inc., 2006), 88-90, 97.

[26] "CPI Inflation Calculator," Bureau of Labor Statistics, U.S. Department of Labor, <http://www.bls.gov/data/inflation_calculator.htm> (20 November 2011).

[27] "A Summary of the 2011 Annual Reports," Status of the Social Security and Medicare Programs, Actuarial Publications, Social Security Online, <http://www.ssa.gov/oact/TRSUM/index.html> (1 December 2011).

[28] "Will You Need LTC?" National Clearinghouse for Long Term Information, U.S. Department of Health and Human Services, <http://www.longtermcare.gov/LTC/Main_Site/Understanding/Definition/Know.aspx> (21 March 2012).

[29] "Emerging Trends and Findings," Executive Summary, Genworth 2011 Cost of Care Survey, <http://www.genworth.com/content/etc/medialib/genworth_v2/pdf/ltc_cost_of_care.Par.85518.File.dat/Executive%20Summary_gnw.pdf> (21 March 2012).

[30] Material discussed is meant for general illustration and/or informational purposes only and it is not to be construed as tax, legal or investment advice.

[31] "U.S. Federal Individual Income Tax Rates History, 1913-2011," Tax Foundation, <http://www.taxfoundation.org/files/fed_individual_rate_history_nominal&adjusted-20110909.pdf> (27 March 2012).

[32] We do not provide tax or legal advice. Please consult the appropriate advisor for more information regarding your specific situation.

[33] We do not provide tax or legal advice. Please consult the appropriate advisor for more information regarding your specific situation.

[34] Napoleon Hill, *Think and Grow Rich: The 21st-Century Edition* (Highroads Media, Inc., 2004), 107.

Made in the USA
San Bernardino, CA
05 July 2016